Doering

The spirit of America that speaks from every page of this beautiful book will stir every American heart. Filled with happy memories, glowing inspiration, and hearty, wholesome reading, this is a perfect fireside book for the whole family—young folks, old folks, dads and mothers—to enjoy together.

To no two people will this collection mean quite the same thing. It is a kind of feast which each one will season with the salt and pepper of his own experience. But wherever one dips into the pages, one will find something richly American in flavor and expression. And blending prose and verse together in one harmonious whole, John Dukes McKee's enchanting illustrations are themselves as American in character as the text.

MY
AMERICAN
HERITAGE

mister mckee

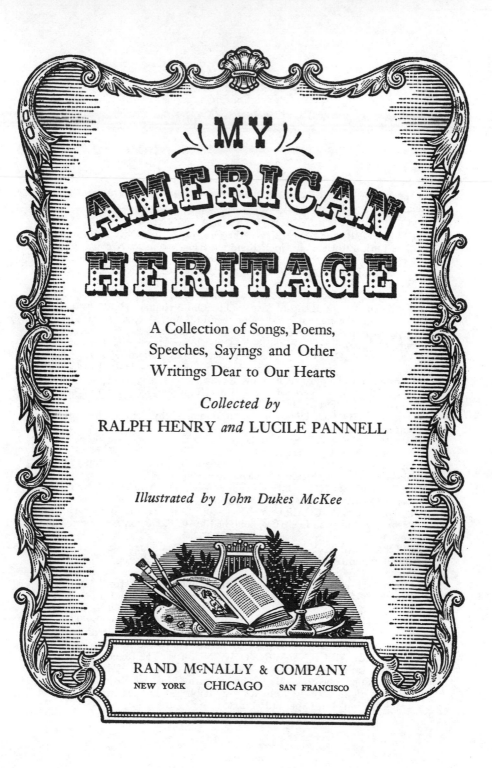

# MY AMERICAN HERITAGE

A Collection of Songs, Poems,
Speeches, Sayings and Other
Writings Dear to Our Hearts

*Collected by*

RALPH HENRY *and* LUCILE PANNELL

*Illustrated by John Dukes McKee*

RAND McNALLY & COMPANY
NEW YORK    CHICAGO    SAN FRANCISCO

### ACKNOWLEDGMENTS

For permission to reprint material copyrighted or otherwise controlled, our thanks are gratefully extended to the following publishers:

APPLETON-CENTURY-CROFTS, EDUCATIONAL DIVISION, MEREDITH CORP.—for "The Elf and the Dormouse," by Oliver Herford, and "The Little Elf-Man," by John Kendrick Bangs, from *St. Nicholas Book of Verse,* copyright 1923 The Century Company; "Fer a Dog," from *David Harum* by Edward Noyes Wescott, copyright by Appleton-Century-Crofts; "What Do We Plant?" from *The Poems of Henry Abbey.*

THE BOBBS-MERRILL COMPANY—for "Little Orphant Annie," "Our Hired Girl," "The Raggedy Man," "The Old Swimmin'-Hole," "When the Frost Is on the Punkin," and "Out to Old Aunt Mary's," from *The Biographical Edition of the Complete Works of James Whitcomb Riley,* copyright 1913, reprinted by permission of the Bobbs-Merrill Co., Inc.

BRANDT & BRANDT—for "Nancy Hanks," from *A Book of Americans* by Rosemary and Stephen Vincent Benét, published by Holt, Rinehart and Winston, Inc. Copyright 1933 by Rosemary and Stephen Vincent Benét, renewal © 1961 by Rosemary Carr Benét. Reprinted by permission of Holt, Rinehart and Winston, Inc.

THE CHICAGO TRIBUNE—for "Injun Summer," by John T. McCutcheon, reprinted, courtesy of the *Chicago Tribune.*

COWARD, McCANN & GEOGHEGAN, INC.—for "Counters," from *Compass Rose* by Elizabeth Coatsworth. Copyright 1929 by Coward-McCann, Inc., renewal © 1957 by Elizabeth Coatsworth. Reprinted by permission of Coward, McCann & Geoghegan, Inc.

DODGE PUBLISHING COMPANY—for "Well, Did You Hear?" by Edward Vance Cooke.

E. P. DUTTON & COMPANY, INC.—for "America the Beautiful," from *Poems,* by Katherine Lee Bates, published by E. P. Dutton & Company, Inc., New York.

FORBES & COMPANY—for "The Pessimist," by Ben King.

HARCOURT BRACE JOVANOVICH, INC.—for "The Fog," from *Chicago Poems* by Carl Sandburg, copyright 1916 by Henry Holt and Company, Inc., copyright 1944 by Carl Sandburg. For "Primer Lesson," from *Slabs of the Sunburnt West* by Carl Sandburg, copyright 1922 by Harcourt Brace Jovanovich, Inc., copyright 1950 by Carl Sandburg, reprinted by permission of the publisher. For "The Young Mystic," copyright 1914 by Harcourt Brace Jovanovich, Inc., copyright 1942 by Louis Untermeyer, reprinted from *Long Feud* by Louis Untermeyer by permission of the publisher.

HOLT, RINEHART AND WINSTON, INC.—for "The Runaway" and "The Pasture," from *The Poetry of Robert Frost,* edited by Edward Connery Lathem. Copyright 1923, 1939, © 1967, 1969 by Holt, Rinehart and Winston, Inc. Copyright 1951 by Robert Frost. Published in the British Commonwealth by Jonathan Cape, Ltd., London.

THE READER'S DIGEST—for "Condensed History Lesson," by Charles A. Beard, contributed by Arthur H. Secord.

THE REILLY AND LEE COMPANY, AN IMPRINT OF THE HENRY REGNERY COMPANY—for "A Boy and His Dog," from the book *Rhymes of Childhood*, by Edgar A. Guest, copyright 1924 by The Reilly and Lee Company, Chicago; for "Home" and "It Couldn't Be Done," from the book *Collected Verse of Edgar A. Guest*, copyright 1934 by The Reilly and Lee Company, Chicago.

SAN FRANCISCO EXAMINER—for "Casey at the Bat," by Ernest Lawrence Thayer.

CHARLES SCRIBNER'S SONS—for "America for Me" and "Four Things," reprinted from *The Poems of Henry van Dyke*, copyright 1911 by Charles Scribner's Sons, 1939 by Tertius van Dyke, used with permission of the publishers; "The Day's Demand," from *The Complete Poetical Writings of J. G. Holland;* "Life, a Question," reprinted from *The Poems of Corinne Roosevelt Robinson*, copyright 1921 by Charles Scribner's Sons, renewal copyright 1949 Corinne R. Alsop, and used by permission of the publishers; "Eternal Partnership," from *Children of the Night* by E. A. Robinson; "The Dinkey-Bird," "The Duel," "Just 'fore Christmas," "The Rock-A-Bye Lady," and "Seein' Things," reprinted from *Love Songs of Childhood* by Eugene Field; "Little Boy Blue" and "Wynken, Blynken, and Nod" from *The Works of Eugene Field;* "The Sugar-Plum Tree," reprinted from *Second Book of Verse* by Eugene Field.

THE VIKING PRESS, INC.—for "The Hens" and "The Rabbit," from *Under the Tree* by Elizabeth Madox Roberts, copyright 1922 by B. W. Huebsch, Inc., 1950 by Ivor S. Roberts. Reprinted by permission of The Viking Press, Inc.

JERRY VOGEL MUSIC CO.—for "Trees," by Joyce Kilmer. Copyright 1913, renewed 1941. Copyright assigned to Jerry Vogel Music Co., Inc., New York. Used by permission of copyright owner. Reproduction prohibited.

YALE UNIVERSITY PRESS—for "The Ambitious Mouse," from *Songs for Parents*, by John Farrar, copyright by Yale University Press.

To the following individuals and organizations our thanks are due for special permission to use their material:

BOY SCOUTS OF AMERICA—for "The Scout Oath."

HELEN K. BRADBURY—for "The Sandman," by Margaret Thomson Janvier (Margaret Vandegrift).

BERTON BRALEY—for "Opportunity," copyright by Berton Braley, all rights reserved.

GIRL SCOUTS OF THE UNITED STATES OF AMERICA—for "The Girl Scout Promise."

EVELYN AND LUCIEN HARRIS—for "Advice to Writers for the Daily Press," by Joel Chandler Harris.

ISABEL GARLAND LORD—for "Do You Fear the Wind?" from *Prairie Songs*, by Hamlin Garland.

LOUIS F. LOVEMAN—for "April Rain," by Robert Loveman.

JUANITA JOAQUINA MILLER—for "Columbus" and "Judge Not," from *The Complete Poetical Works of Joaquin Miller*.

ROBERT NATHAN—for "The Daughter at Evening," from *Youth Grows Old* by Robert Nathan, published by Alfred A. Knopf, Inc.

JOHN D. ROCKEFELLER, JR.—for "I Believe."

Dedicated with love
to the men and women
who wrote this book

*Personal Acknowledgments*

For their assistance the compilers are grateful to

    *Marie Barkman,* Mead Library

    *Frances Cavanah,* author and editor

    *Herma Clark,* author and columnist

    *Genevieve Foster,* author and illustrator

    *Emma B. Henry,* La Grange, Illinois

    *Marguerite Henry,* author

    *Ellen L. Knight,* Chicago, Illinois

    *Mary G. Lusson,* Director of Division of Curriculum Development, Chicago Public Schools

    *Dilla W. MacBean,* Director of the Division of Libraries, Chicago Public Schools

    *Alice R. Brooks McGuire,* Materials Center, University of Chicago

    *Mearle J. Pannell,* Elmhurst, Illinois

    *Sigrid Sittig,* Lombard, Illinois

    *Ruth Strand,* Elmhurst Public Library

    *M. Bernard Tietze,* San Gabriel, California

    *Gertrude Zochert,* Lloyd School Library

RALPH HENRY
LUCILE PANNELL

1    CHILDHOOD    *19*

2    YOUTH    *85*

3    AMERICA    *153*

INDEX    *291*

# INTRODUCTION

There are hours of delight in this book for Americans of any age.

No lover of books, however well along in years, can resist the appeal of old favorites reread. And no up-and-coming boy or girl, blessed with the tender, green-leafed sagacity of the young, ever fails to recognize the magic of verses like James Whitcomb Riley's "Little Orphant Annie."

Now this is not to suggest that "Little Orphant Annie" is one of the great poems in literature—or that this book is a collection intended primarily for boys and girls. Nor is it to say that the collection presents only the "best" of the American literary heritage.

Obviously, much of that excellent "best" has been included by the editors. But quite as obviously, a number of sentimental relics, ripe old chestnuts, and dear old platitudes have also been included.

In short, grownups and children alike will find here some of the finest American prose and verse—from Emerson and Thoreau to Carl Sandburg and Robert Frost—and some of the most humble and unpretentious. They will find the sense and sensibility of ten generations of American life—ballads, songs, apothegms, nursery rhymes, letters, jokes, love lyrics, political wisdom. Young enough, they will read things they have never read before, and thus experience the incomparable joys of discovery. Old enough, they will smile and relax under the heartwarming spell of the familiar.

> *Then read from the treasured volume*
> *The poem of thy choice,*
> *And lend to the rhyme of the poet*
> *The beauty of thy voice.*
>
> *And the night shall be filled with music*
> *And the cares that infest the day,*
> *Shall fold their tents, like the Arabs,*
> *And as silently steal away.*

# ~1~
# CHILDHOOD

mister mckee

## ADVENTURE

### Anonymous

Here's an adventure! what awaits
Beyond these closed, mysterious gates?
Whom shall I meet, where shall I go?
Beyond the lovely land I know?
Above the sky, across the sea?
What shall I learn and feel and be?
Open, strange doors, to good or ill!
I hold my breath a moment still
Before the magic of your look.
What shall you do to me, O Book?

## THE AMBITIOUS MOUSE

### John Farrar

If all the world were candy
    And the sky were frosted cake,
Oh, it would be a splendid job
    For a mouse to undertake!

To eat a path of sweetmeats
    Through candy forest aisles—

Explore the land of Peppermint
   Stretched out for miles and miles.

To gobble up a cloudlet,
   A little cup-cake star,
To swim a lake of liquid sweet
   With shores of chocolate bar.

But best of all the eating,
   Would be the toothsome, fat,
Triumphant hour of mouse-desire,
   To eat a candy cat!

## IT WAS

### Dorothy Aldis

When he came to tuck me in
And pat me on the head
He tried to guess (he always does)
Who was in my bed.

"Is it Sally?" he guessed first,
"Or her sister Joan?
   It's such a wriggling little girl
   It couldn't be my own.

"It can't be Mary Ann," he said,
"Or Deborah because
   All their eyes are much too blue—
   *My goodness me, I think it's you!*"
   And he was right. It was.

# THE DAUGHTER AT EVENING
### Robert Nathan

Before her supper where she sits
With every favored toe she plays,
Singing whatever ballad fits
The past romances of her days.

The dusk comes softly to her room,
The night winds in the branches stir,
That nations battle to their doom
Across the seas, is naught to her.

For what she does not know, she eats,
A worm, a twig, a block, a fly,
And every novel thing she meets
Is bitten into bye and bye.

She, from the blankets of her bed,
Holds no opinion on the war,
But munches on her thumb instead,
This being what a thumb is for.

The troubles that invade the day,
On some remote tomorrow creep;
Comes Bertha with the supper tray,
And—now I laymen down ee beep.

[ 21 ]

## THE BROWN THRUSH

Lucy Larcom

There's a merry brown thrush sitting up in the tree.
"He's singing to me! He's singing to me!"
　　And what does he say, little girl, little boy?
　"Oh, the world's running over with joy!
　　　Don't you hear? Don't you see?
　　　Hush! Look! In my tree,
　　　I'm as happy as happy can be!"

And the brown thrush keeps singing, "A nest do you see,
And five eggs hid by me in the juniper tree?
　　Don't meddle! Don't touch! little girl, little boy,
　Or the world will lose some of its joy!
　　　Now I'm glad! Now I'm free!
　　　And I always shall be,
　　　If you never bring sorrow to me."

So the merry brown thrush sings away in the tree,
To you and to me, to you and to me;
　　And he sings all the day, little girl, little boy,
　"Oh, the world's running over with joy!
　　　But long it won't be,
　　　Don't you know? Don't you see?
　　　Unless you're as good as can be."

# ANIMAL CRACKERS

### Christopher Morley

Animal crackers, and cocoa to drink,
That is the finest of suppers, I think;
When I'm grown up and can have what I please
I think I shall always insist upon these. . . .

—Selected from "Animal Crackers"

## MY NOSE

### Dorothy Aldis

It doesn't breathe;
It doesn't smell;
It doesn't feel
So very well.

I am discouraged
With my nose:
The only thing it
Does is blows.

# THE DIFFERENCE

Laura Elizabeth Richards

Eight fingers,
Ten toes,
Two eyes,
And one nose.
Baby said
When she smelt the rose,
"Oh, what a pity
I've only one nose!"

Ten teeth
In even rows,
Three dimples,
And one nose.
Baby said
When she smelt snuff,
"Deary me!
One nose is enough!"

# THE LITTLE ELF-MAN

John Kendrick Bangs

I met a little Elf-man, once,
  Down where the lilies blow.
I asked him why he was so small,
  And why he didn't grow.

He slightly frowned, and with his eye
  He looked me through and through.
"I'm quite as big for me," said he,
  "As you are big for you."

# A BOY AND HIS DOG

### Edgar A. Guest

A boy and his dog make a glorious pair;
No better friendship is found anywhere,
For they talk and they walk and they run and they play,
And they have their deep secrets for many a day;
And that boy has a comrade who thinks and who feels,
Who walks down the road with a dog at his heels.

He may go where he will and his dog will be there,
May revel in mud and his dog will not care;
Faithful he'll stay for the highest command
And bark with delight at the touch of his hand;
Oh, he owns a treasure which nobody steals,
Who walks down the road with a dog at his heels.

No other can lure him away from his side;
He's proof against riches and station and pride;
Fine dress does not charm him, and flattery's breath
Is lost on the dog, for he's faithful to death;
He sees the great soul which the body conceals—
Oh, it's great to be young with a dog at your heels!

[ 25 ]

# THE CHILDREN'S HOUR

### Henry Wadsworth Longfellow

Between the dark and the daylight,
   When the night is beginning to lower,
Comes a pause in the day's occupations
   That is known as the Children's Hour.

I hear in the chamber above me
   The patter of little feet,
The sound of a door that is opened,
   And voices soft and sweet.

From my study I see in the lamplight,
   Descending the broad hall stair,
Grave Alice, and laughing Allegra,
   And Edith with golden hair.

A whisper, and then a silence:
   Yet I know by their merry eyes
They are plotting and planning together
   To take me by surprise.

A sudden rush from the stairway,
   A sudden raid from the hall!
By three doors left unguarded
   They enter my castle wall!

They climb up into my turret
   O'er the arms and back of my chair;
If I try to escape, they surround me;
   They seem to be everywhere.

They almost devour me with kisses,
   Their arms about me entwine,

Till I think of the Bishop of Bingen
    In his Mouse-Tower on the Rhine!

Do you think, O blue-eyed banditti,
    Because you have scaled the wall,
Such an old mustache as I am
    Is not a match for you all!

I have you fast in my fortress,
    And will not let you depart,
But put you down into the dungeon
    In the round-tower of my heart.

And there will I keep you forever,
    Yes, forever and a day,
Till the walls shall crumble to ruin,
    And moulder in dust away!

## GOOD NIGHT

Samuel Griswold Goodrich (Peter Parley)

The sun has sunk behind the hills,
    The shadows o'er the landscape creep;
A drowsy sound the woodland fills,
    As nature folds her arms to sleep:
        Good night—good night.

            —Selected from "Good Night"

## WE THANK THEE

Anonymous

For mother-love and father-care,
For brothers strong and sisters fair,
For love at home and here each day,
For guidance lest we go astray,
    Father in Heaven, we thank Thee.

For this new morning with its light,
For rest and shelter of the night,
For health and food, for love and friends,
For ev'rything His goodness sends,
    Father in Heaven, we thank Thee.

For flowers that bloom about our feet,
For tender grass, so fresh, so sweet,
For song of bird and hum of bee,
For all things fair we hear or see,
    Father in Heaven, we thank Thee.

For blue of stream and blue of sky,
For pleasant shade of branches high,
For fragrant air and cooling breeze,
For beauty of the blooming trees,
    Father in Heaven, we thank Thee.

# THE BAREFOOT BOY

John Greenleaf Whittier

Blessings on thee, little man,
Barefoot boy, with cheek of tan!
With thy turned-up pantaloons,
And thy merry whistled tunes;
With thy red lip, redder still
Kissed by strawberries on the hill;
With the sunshine on thy face,
Through thy torn brim's jaunty grace;
From my heart I give thee joy—
I was once a barefoot boy!

Oh for boyhood's painless play,
Sleep that wakes in laughing day,
Health that mocks the doctor's rules,
Knowledge never learned of schools,

\* \* \*

For, eschewing books and tasks,
Nature answers all he asks;
Hand in hand with her he walks,
Face to face with her he talks,
Part and parcel of her joy—
Blessings on thee, barefoot boy!

—Selected from "The Barefoot Boy"

## THE DINKEY-BIRD

Eugene Field

In an ocean, 'way out yonder
　(As all sapient people know),
Is the land of Wonder-Wander,
　Whither children love to go;
It's their playing, romping, swinging,
　That give great joy to me
While the Dinkey-Bird goes singing
　In the amfalula tree!

There the gum-drops grow like cherries
　And taffy's thick as peas—
Caramels you pick like berries
　When, and where, and how you please;
Big red sugar-plums are clinging
　To the cliffs beside that sea
Where the Dinkey-Bird is singing
　In the amfalula tree.

So when children shout and scamper
　And make merry all the day,

When there's naught to put a damper
  To the ardor of their play;
When I hear their laughter ringing,
  Then I'm sure as sure can be
That the Dinkey-Bird is singing
  In the amfalula tree.

—Selected from "The Dinkey-Bird"

## THERE WAS A LITTLE GIRL

### Anonymous

There was a little girl,
And she had a little curl
Right in the middle of her forehead.
When she was good
She was very, very good,
And when she was bad she was horrid.

One day she went upstairs,
When her parents, unawares,
In the kitchen were occupied with meals,
And she stood upon her head
In her little trundle-bed,
And then began hooraying with her heels.

Her mother heard the noise,
And she thought it was the boys
A-playing at a combat in the attic;
But when she climbed the stair,
And found Jemima there,
She took and she did spank her most emphatic.

—(Sometimes attributed to Henry Wadsworth Longfellow)

## LITTLE THINGS

Ebenezer Cobham Brewer

Little drops of water,
Little grains of sand,
Make the mighty ocean
And the pleasant land.

Little deeds of kindness,
Little words of love,
Help to make earth happy
Like the heaven above.

—Selected from "Little Things"

## THE ORIGIN OF
## THE FORGET-ME-NOT

Emily Bruce Roelofson

When to the flowers so beautiful
  The Father gave a name,
Back came a little blue-eyed one
  (All timidly it came);
And standing at its Father's feet
  And gazing in His face,
It said, in low and trembling tone,
  And yet with gentle grace,
"Dear God, the name Thou gavest me,
  Alas! I have forgot!"
Kindly the Father looked Him down
  And said: "Forget-me-not."

# THE HENS

### Elizabeth Madox Roberts

The night was coming very fast;
It reached the gate as I ran past.

The pigeons had gone to the tower of the church
And all the hens were on their perch,

Up in the barn, and I thought I heard
A piece of a little purring word.

I stopped inside, waiting and staying,
To try to hear what the hens were saying.

They were asking something, that was plain,
Asking it over and over again.

One of them moved and turned around,
Her feathers made a ruffled sound,

A ruffled sound, like a bushful of birds,
And she said her little asking words.

She pushed her head close into her wing,
But nothing answered anything.

# THE DUEL

### Eugene Field

The gingham dog and the calico cat
Side by side on the table sat;
'Twas half past twelve, and (what do you think!)
Nor one nor t'other had slept a wink!
  The old Dutch clock and the Chinese plate
  Appeared to know as sure as fate
There was going to be a terrible spat.
      *(I wasn't there; I simply state*
      *What was told to me by the Chinese plate!)*

The gingham dog went "bow-wow-wow!"
And the calico cat replied "mee-ow!"
The air was littered, an hour or so,
With bits of gingham and calico.
  While the old Dutch clock in the chimney place
  Up with its hands before its face,
For it always dreaded a family row!
      *(Now mind; I'm only telling you*
      *What the old Dutch clock declares is true!)*

The Chinese plate looked very blue,
And wailed, "Oh, dear! what shall we do!"
But the gingham dog and the calico cat
Wallowed this way and tumbled that,
  Employing every tooth and claw
  In the awfullest way you ever saw—
And, oh! how the gingham and calico flew!
      *(Don't fancy I exaggerate—*
      *I got my news from the Chinese plate!)*

Next morning, where the two had sat
They found no trace of dog or cat;

And some folks think unto this day
That burglars stole that pair away!
  But the truth about the cat and pup
  Is this: they ate each other up!
Now what do you really think of that!
    *(The old Dutch clock it told me so,
    And that is how I came to know.)*

## FOUR-LEAF CLOVER

Ella Higginson

I know a place where the sun is like gold,
  And the cherry blossoms burst with snow,
And down underneath is the loveliest nook,
  Where the four-leaf clovers grow.

One leaf is for hope, and one is for faith,
  And one is for love, you know,
And God put another in for luck—
  If you search, you will find where they grow.

But you must have hope, and you must have faith,
  You must love and be strong—and so
If you work, if you wait, you will find the place
  Where the four-leaf clovers grow.

## INJUN SUMMER
### John T. McCutcheon

Yep, sonny, this is sure enough Injun summer. Don't know what that is, I reckon, do you?

Well, that's when all the homesick Injuns come back to play. You know, a long time ago, long afore yer granddaddy was born even, there used to be heaps of Injuns around here—thousands—millions, I reckon, far as that's concerned. Reg'lar sure 'nough Injuns—none o' yer cigar store Injuns, not much. They wuz all around here—right here where you're standin'.

Don't be skeered—hain't none around here now, leastways no live ones. They been gone this many a year.

They all went away and died, so they ain't no more left.

But every year, 'long about now, they all come back, leastways their sperrits do. They're here now. You can see 'em off across the fields. Look real hard. See that kind o' hazy, misty look out yonder? Well, them's Injuns—Injun sperrits marchin' along an' dancin' in the sunlight. That's what makes that kind o' haze that's everywhere—it's jest the sperrits of the Injuns all come back. They're all around us now.

See off yonder; see them tepees? They kind o' look like corn shocks from here, but them's Injun tents, sure as you're a foot high. See 'em now? Sure, I knowed you could. Smell that smoky sort o' smell in the air? That's the campfires a-burnin' and their pipes a-goin'.

Lots o' people say it's jest leaves burnin', but it ain't. It's the campfires, an' th' Injuns are hoppin' 'round 'em t' beat the old Harry.

You jest come out here tonight when the moon is hangin' over the hill off yonder an' the harvest fields is all swimmin' in the moonlight, an' you can see the Injuns and the tepees jest as plain as kin be. You can, eh? I knowed you would after a little while.

Jever notice how the leaves turn red 'bout this time o' year? That's jest another sign o' redskins. That's when an old Injun sperrit gits tired dancin' an' goes up an' squats on a leaf t' rest. Why, I kin hear 'em rustlin' an' whisperin' an' creepin' 'round among the leaves all the time; an' ever' once'n a while a leaf gives way under some fat old Injun ghost and comes floatin' down to the ground. See—here's one now. See how red it is? That's the war paint rubbed off'n an Injun ghost, sure's you're born.

Purty soon all the Injuns 'll go marchin' away agin, back to the happy huntin' grounds, but next year you'll see 'em troopin' back— th' sky jest hazy with 'em and their campfires smolderin' away jest like they are now.

—From *The Chicago Tribune* of September 30, 1907

## TO THE DANDELION
James Russell Lowell

Dear common flower, that grow'st beside the way,
Fringing the dusty road with harmless gold.

—Selected from "To the Dandelion"

## BEAUTIFUL

Anonymous

Beautiful faces are they that wear
The light of a pleasant spirit there;
Beautiful hands are they that do
Deeds that are noble, good and true;
Beautiful feet are they that go
Swiftly to lighten another's woe.

—From *McGuffey's Second Reader*


## PERSEVERE

Anonymous

The fisher who draws in his net too soon,
   Won't have any fish to sell;
The child who shuts up his book too soon,
   Won't learn any lessons well.

If you would have your learning stay,
   Be patient—don't learn too fast;
The man who travels a mile each day,
   May get round the world at last.

—From *McGuffey's Third Reader*

## LITTLE GUSTAVA

Celia Thaxter

Little Gustava sits in the sun,
Safe in the porch, and the little drops run
From the icicles under the eaves so fast,
For the bright spring sun shines warm at last,
    And glad is little Gustava.

She wears a quaint little scarlet cap,
And a little green bowl she holds in her lap,
Filled with bread and milk to the brim,
And a wreath of marigolds round the rim:
    "Ha! ha!" laughs little Gustava.

Up comes her little gray coaxing cat
With her little pink nose, and she mews, "What's that?"
Gustava feeds her—she begs for more;
And a little brown hen walks in at the door:
    "Good day!" cries little Gustava.

She scatters crumbs for the little brown hen.
There comes a rush and a flutter, and then
Down fly her little white doves so sweet,
With their snowy wings and crimson feet:
    "Welcome!" cries little Gustava.

So dainty and eager they pick up the crumbs;
But who is this through the doorway comes?
Little Scotch terrier, little dog Rags,
Looks in her face, and his funny tail wags:
    "Ha! ha!" laughs little Gustava.

"You want some breakfast too?" and down
She sets her bowl on the brick floor brown;
And little dog Rags drinks up her milk,
While she strokes his shaggy locks like silk:
    "Dear Rags!" says little Gustava.

Waiting without stood sparrow and crow,
Cooling their feet in the melting snow:
"Won't you come in, good folk?" she cried.
But they were too bashful, and stood outside
        Though "Pray come in!" cried Gustava.

So the last she threw them, and knelt on the mat
With doves and biddy and dog and cat.
And her mother came to the open house-door:
"Dear little daughter, I bring you some more,
    My merry little Gustava!"

Kitty and terrier, biddy and doves,
All things harmless Gustava loves.
The shy, kind creatures 'tis joy to feed,
And oh, her breakfast is sweet indeed
    To happy little Gustava!

# LITTLE BOY BLUE

Eugene Field

The little toy dog is covered with dust,
    But sturdy and stanch he stands;
And the little toy soldier is red with rust,
    And his musket molds in his hands.
Time was when the little toy dog was new
    And the soldier was passing fair;
And that was the time when our Little Boy Blue
    Kissed them and put them there.

"Now, don't you go till I come," he said,
    "And don't you make any noise!"
So, toddling off to his trundle-bed,
    He dreamed of the pretty toys;
And as he was dreaming, an angel song
    Awakened our Little Boy Blue—
Oh! the years are many, the years are long,
    But the little toy friends are true!

Aye, faithful to Little Boy Blue they stand,
    Each in the same old place—
Awaiting the touch of a little hand,
    And the smile of a little face;
And they wonder, as waiting these long years through
    In the dust of that little chair,
What has become of our Little Boy Blue,
    Since he kissed them and put them there.

# IS THERE A SANTA CLAUS?

Francis Pharcellus Church

We take pleasure in answering at once and thus prominently the communication below, expressing at the same time our great gratification that its faithful author is numbered among the friends of *The Sun:*

> DEAR EDITOR—I am eight years old. Some of my little friends say there is no Santa Claus. Papa says "If you see it in *The Sun*, it's so." Please tell me the truth; is there a Santa Claus?
>
> VIRGINIA O'HANLON
> 115 W. Ninety-fifth Street

Virginia, your little friends are wrong. They have been affected by the skepticism of a skeptical age. They do not believe except they see. They think that nothing can be which is not comprehensible by their little minds. All minds, Virginia, whether they be men's or children's, are little. In this great universe of ours man is a mere insect, an ant, in his intellect, as compared with the boundless world about him, as measured by the intelligence capable of grasping the whole of truth and knowledge.

Yes, Virginia, there is a Santa Claus. He exists as certainly as love and generosity and devotion exist, and you know that they abound and give to your life its highest beauty and joy. Alas! how dreary would be the world if there were no Santa Claus. It would be as dreary as if there were no Virginias. There would be no childlike faith then, no poetry, no romance to make tolerable this existence. We should have no enjoyment, except in sense and sight. The eternal light with which childhood fills the world would be extinguished.

Not believe in Santa Claus! You might as well not believe in fairies! You might get your papa to hire men to watch in all the chimneys on Christmas Eve to catch Santa Claus, but even if they did not see Santa Claus coming down, what would that prove? Nobody sees Santa Claus, but that is no sign that there is no Santa Claus. The most real things in the world are those that neither children nor men can see. Did you ever see fairies dancing on the lawn? Of course not, but that's no proof that they are not there. Nobody can conceive or imagine all the wonders there are unseen and unseeable in the world.

You may tear apart the baby's rattle and see what makes the noise inside, but there is a veil covering the unseen world which not the strongest man, nor even the united strength of all the strongest men that ever lived, could tear apart. Only faith, fancy, poetry, love, romance, can push aside that curtain and view and picture the supernal beauty and glory beyond. Is it all real? Ah, Virginia, in all this world there is nothing else real and abiding.

No Santa Claus! Thank God! he lives, and he lives forever. A thousand years from now, Virginia, nay, ten times ten thousand years from now, he will continue to make glad the heart of childhood.

—From the *New York Sun* of September 21, 1897

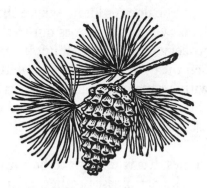

## JEST 'FORE CHRISTMAS

Eugene Field

Father calls me William, sister calls me Will,
Mother calls me Willie, but the fellers call me Bill!
Mighty glad I ain't a girl—ruther be a boy,
Without them sashes, curls, an' things that's worn by Fauntleroy!
Love to chawnk green apples an' go swimmin' in the lake—
Hate to take the castor-ile they give for belly-ache!
'Most all the time, the whole year round, there ain't no flies on me,
But jest 'fore Christmas I'm as good as I kin be!

Got a yeller dog named Sport, sick him on a cat;
First thing she knows she doesn't know where she is at!
Got a clipper sled, an' when us kids goes out to slide,
Long comes the grocery cart, an' we all hook a ride!
But sometimes when the grocery man is worrited an' cross,
He reaches at us with his whip, an' larrups up his hoss,
An' then I laff and holler, "Oh, ye never teched me!"
But jest 'fore Christmas I'm as good as I kin be!

Gran'ma says she hopes that when I git to be a man,
I'll be a missionarer like her oldest brother, Dan,

[ 44 ]

As was et up by the cannibuls that lives in Ceylon's Isle,
Where every prospeck pleases, an' only man is vile!
But gran'ma she has never been to see a Wild West show,
Nor read the Life of Daniel Boone, or else I guess she'd know
That Buff'lo Bill an' cowboys is good enough for me!
*Excep'* jest 'fore Christmas when I'm good as I kin be!

And then old Sport he hangs around, so solemn-like an' still
His eyes they seem a'sayin': "What's the matter, little Bill?"
The old cat sneaks down off her perch an' wonders what's become
Of them two enemies of hern that used to make things hum!
But I am so perlite an' tend so earnestly to biz,
That mother says to father: "How improved our Willie is!"
But father, havin' been a boy hisself, suspicions me
When, jest 'fore Christmas I'm as good as I kin be!

For Christmas, with its lots an' lots of candies, cakes, an' toys,
Was made, they say, for proper kids an' not for naughty boys;
So wash yer face an' bresh yer hair, an' mind yer p's an' q's,
An' don't bust out yer pantaloons, an' don't wear out yer shoes;
Say "Yessum" to the ladies, an' "Yessur" to the men,
An' when they's company, don't pass yer plate for pie again;
But, thinkin' of the things yer'd like to see upon that tree,
Jest 'fore Christmas be as good as yer kin be!

## LITTLE ORPHANT ANNIE

### James Whitcomb Riley

Little Orphant Annie's come to our house to stay,
An' wash the cups an' saucers up, an' brush the crumbs away,
An' shoo the chickens off the porch, an' dust the hearth, an' sweep,
An' make the fire, an' bake the bread, an' earn her board-an'-keep;
An' all us other children, when the supper things is done,
We set around the kitchen fire an' has the mostest fun
A-list'nin' to the witch-tales 'at Annie tells about,
An' the Gobble-uns 'at gits you

Ef you
Don't
Watch
Out!

Onc't they was a little boy wouldn't say his prayers—
An' when he went to bed at night, away upstairs,
His Mammy heerd him holler, an' his Daddy heerd him bawl,
An' when they turn't the kivvers down, he wasn't there at all!
An' they seeked him in the rafter-room, an' cubby-hole, an' press,
An' seeked him up the chimbly-flue, an' ever'-wheres, I guess;

But all they ever found wuz jist his pants an' roundabout:—
An' the Gobble-uns'll git you
                Ef you
            Don't
                Watch
                    Out!

An' one time a little girl 'ud allus laugh an' grin,
An' make fun of ever' one, an' all her blood-an'-kin;
An' onc't when they was "company," an' ole folks wuz there,
She mocked 'em, an' shocked 'em, an' said she didn't care!
An' thist as she kicked her heels, an' turn't to run an' hide,
They wuz two great big Black Things a-standin' by her side,
An' they snatched her through the ceilin' 'fore she knowed
        what she's about!
An' the Gobble-uns'll git you
                Ef you
            Don't
                Watch
                    Out!

An' little Orphant Annie says, when the blaze is blue,
An' the lampwick sputters, an' the wind goes *woo-oo!*
An' you hear the crickets quit, an' the moon is gray,
An' the lightnin'-bugs in dew is all squenched away,—
You better mind yer parents, and yer teachers fond an' dear,
An' cherish them 'at loves you, an' dry the orphant's tear,
An' he'p the pore an' needy ones 'at clusters all about,
Er the Gobble-uns'll git *you*
                Ef you
            Don't
                Watch
                    Out!

# THE ROCK-A-BY LADY

Eugene Field

The Rock-a-By Lady from Hushaby street
　　Comes stealing; comes creeping;
The poppies they hang from her head to her feet,
And each hath a dream that is tiny and fleet—
She bringeth her poppies to you, my sweet,
　　When she findeth you sleeping!

There is one little dream of a beautiful drum—
　　"Rub-a-dub!" it goeth;
There is one little dream of a big sugar-plum,
And lo! thick and fast the other dreams come
Of popguns that bang, and tin tops that hum,
　　And a trumpet that bloweth!

And dollies peep out of those wee little dreams
　　With laughter and singing;
And boats go a-floating on silvery streams,
And the stars peek-a-boo with their own misty gleams,
And up, up, and up, where the Mother Moon beams,
　　The fairies go winging!

Would you dream all these dreams that are tiny and fleet?
　　They'll come to you sleeping;
So shut the two eyes that are weary, my sweet,
For the Rock-a-By Lady from Hushaby street,
With poppies that hang from her head to her feet,
　　Comes stealing; comes creeping.

# THE LITTLE PEOPLE

### (Attributed to John Greenleaf Whittier)

A dreary place would be this earth,
   Were there no little people in it;
The song of life would lose its mirth,
   Were there no children to begin it;

No little forms, like buds to grow,
   And make the admiring heart surrender;
No little hands on breast and brow,
   To keep the thrilling love chords tender.

The sterner souls would grow more stern,
   Unfeeling nature more inhuman,
And man to utter coldness turn,
   And woman would be less than woman.

Life's song, indeed, would lose its charm,
   Were there no babies to begin it;
A doleful place this world would be,
   Were there no little people in it.

            —From *McGuffey's Third Reader*

## THE ELF AND THE DORMOUSE

Oliver Herford

Under a toadstool crept a wee Elf,
Out of the rain, to shelter himself.

Under the toadstool sound asleep,
Sat a big Dormouse all in a heap.

Trembled the wee Elf, frightened, and yet
Fearing to fly away lest he get wet.

To the next shelter—maybe a mile!
Sudden the wee Elf smiled a wee smile,

Tugged till the toadstool toppled in two.
Holding it over him, gayly he flew.

Soon he was safe home, dry as could be.
Soon woke the Dormouse—"Good gracious me!

"Where is my toadstool?" loud he lamented.
—And that's how umbrellas first were invented.

# BABY-LAND

### George Cooper

"Which is the way to Baby-land?"
  "Any one can tell;
      Up one flight,
      To your right;
  Please to ring the bell."

"What can you see in Baby-land?"
  "Little folks in white,
      Downy heads,
      Cradle-beds,
  Faces pure and bright!"

"What do they do in Baby-land?"
  "Dream and wake and play,
      Laugh and crow,
      Shout and grow,
  Jolly times have they!"

"What do they say in Baby-land?"
  "Why, the oddest things;
      Might as well
      Try to tell
  What a birdie sings!"

"Who is the Queen of Baby-land?"
  "Mother, kind and sweet;
      And her love,
      Born above,
  Guides the little feet."

## OUR HIRED GIRL
### James Whitcomb Riley

Our hired girl, she's 'Lizabuth Ann;
　An' she can cook best things to eat!
She ist puts dough in our pie-pan,
　An' pours in somepin' 'at's good an' sweet;
An' nen she salts it all on top
With cinnamon; an' nen she'll stop
　An' stoop an' slide it, ist as slow,
In th' old cook-stove, so's 'twon't slop
　An' git all spilled; nen bakes it, so
　It's custard-pie, first thing you know!
　　An' nen she'll say,
　"Clear out o' my way!
　　They's time fer work, an' time fer play!—
　　　Take yer dough, an' run, child, run!
　　　Er I cain't git no cookin' done!"

When our hired girl 'tends like she's mad,
　An' says folks got to walk the chalk
When *she's* around, er wisht they had!
　I play out on our porch an' talk
To Th' Raggedy Man 'at mows our lawn;
An' he says, "Whew!" an' nen leans on

His old crook-scythe, and blinks his eyes,
An' sniffs all 'round an' says, "I swan!
  Ef my old nose don't tell me lies,
  It 'pears like I smell custard-pies!"
    An' nen *he'll* say,
  "Clear out o' my way!
    They's time fer work, an' time fer play!
      Take yer dough, an' run, child, run!
      Er she cain't git no cookin' done!"

Wunst our hired girl, when she
  Got the supper, an' we all et,
An' it wuz night, an' Ma an' me
  An' Pa went wher' the "Social" met,—
An' nen when we come home, an' see
A light in the kitchen-door, an' we
  Heerd a maccordeun, Pa says, "Lan'-
O'Gracious! who can *her* beau be?"
  An' I marched in, an' 'Lizabuth Ann
  Wuz parchin' corn fer The Raggedy Man!
    *Better* say,
  "Clear out o' the way!
    They's time fer work, an' time fer play!
      Take the hint, an' run, child, run!
      Er we cain't git no courtin' done!"

# THE RAGGEDY MAN

### James Whitcomb Riley

O The Raggedy Man! He works fer Pa;
An' he's the goodest man ever you saw!
He comes to our house every day,
An' waters the horses, an' feeds 'em hay;
An' he opens the shed—an' we all ist laugh
When he drives out our little old wobbely calf;
An' nen—ef our hired girl says he can—
He milks the cow fer 'Lizabuth Ann.—
    Ain't he a' awful good Raggedy Man?
      Raggedy! Raggedy! Raggedy Man!

W'y, The Raggedy Man—he's ist so good,
He splits the kindlin' an' chops the wood;
An' nen he spades in our garden, too,
An' does most things 'at *boys* can't do.—
He clumbed clean up in our big tree
An' shook a' apple down fer me—
An' nother'n', too, fer 'Lizabuth Ann—
An' nother'n, too, fer The Raggedy Man.—
    Ain't he a' awful kind Raggedy Man?
      Raggedy! Raggedy! Raggedy Man!

An' The Raggedy Man, he knows most rhymes,
An' tells 'em, ef I be good, sometimes:
Knows 'bout Giunts, an' Griffuns, an' Elves,
An' the Squidgicums-Squees 'at swaller therselves:
An', wite by the pump in our pasture-lot,
He showed me the hole 'at the Wunks is got,
'At lives 'way deep in the ground, an' can
Turn into me, er 'Lizabuth Ann!
    Ain't he a funny old Raggedy Man?
      Raggedy! Raggedy! Raggedy Man!

The Raggedy Man—one time, when he
Wuz makin' a little bow-'n'-orry fer me,
Says, "When you're big like your Pa is,
Air *you* go' to keep a fine store like his—
An' be a rich merchunt—an' wear fine clothes?—
Er what *air* you go' to be, goodness knows?"
An' nen he laughed at 'Lizabuth Ann,
An' I says, " 'M go' to be a Raggedy Man!
  I'm ist go' to be a nice Raggedy Man!"
    Raggedy! Raggedy! Raggedy Man!

## TALL OAKS FROM LITTLE ACORNS

David Everett

You'd scarce expect one of my age
To speak in public on the stage;
And if I chance to fall below
Demosthenes or Cicero,
Don't view me with a critic's eye,
But pass my imperfections by.
Large streams from little fountains flow,
Tall oaks from little acorns grow.

—Selected from "Tall Oaks from Little Acorns Grow"

# THE MOUNTAIN AND THE SQUIRREL

### Ralph Waldo Emerson

The mountain and the squirrel
Had a quarrel,
And the former called the latter "Little prig";
Bun replied,
"You are doubtless very big;
But all sorts of things and weather
Must be taken in together
To make up a year,
And a sphere.
And I think it no disgrace
To occupy my place.
If I'm not so large as you,
You are not so small as I,
And not half so spry.
I'll not deny you make
A very pretty squirrel track.
Talents differ; all is well and wisely put;
If I cannot carry forests on my back,
Neither can you crack a nut!"

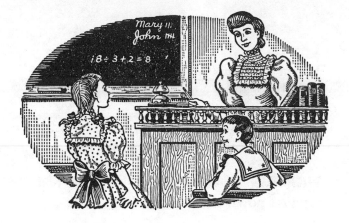

## A MORTIFYING MISTAKE

### Anna Maria Pratt

I studied my tables over and over, and backward and forward, too;
But I couldn't remember six times nine, and I didn't know
    what to do,
Till sister told me to play with my doll, and not to bother my head.
"If you call her 'Fifty-four' for a while, you'll learn it by heart,"
    she said.

So I took my favorite, Mary Ann (though I thought 'twas a
    dreadful shame
To give such a perfectly lovely child such a perfectly horrid name),
And I called her my dear little 'Fifty-four' a hundred times,
    till I knew
The answer of six times nine as well as the answer of two times two.

Next day Elizabeth Wigglesworth, who always acts so proud,
Said "Six times nine is fifty-two," and I nearly laughed aloud!
But I wished I hadn't when teacher said, "Now, Dorothy, tell if
    you can."
For I thought of my doll and—sakes alive!—I answered,
    *"Mary Ann!"*

## THE RABBIT
### Elizabeth Madox Roberts

When they said the time to hide was mine,
I hid back under a thick grape vine.

And while I was still for the time to pass,
A little gray thing came out of the grass.

He hopped his way through the melon bed
And sat down close by a cabbage head.

He sat down close where I could see,
And his big still eyes looked hard at me,

His big eyes bursting out of the rim,
And I looked back very hard at him.

## WORK WHILE YOU WORK
### Anonymous

Work while you work,
   Play while you play;
One thing each time,
   That is the way.
All that you do,
   Do with your might;
Things done by halves
   Are not done right.

—From *McGuffey's Primer*

## MARY'S LAMB

Sarah Josepha Hale

Mary had a little lamb,
  Its fleece was white as snow;
And everywhere that Mary went,
  The lamb was sure to go.
He followed her to school one day,
  Which was against the rule;
It made the children laugh and play
  To see a lamb at school.

And so the teacher turned him out,
  But still he lingered near,
And waited patiently about
  Till Mary did appear.
Then he ran to her, and laid
  His head upon her arm,
As if he said, "I'm not afraid—
  You'll keep me from all harm."

"What makes the lamb love Mary so?"
  The eager children cried.
"Oh, Mary loves the lamb, you know,"
  The teacher quick replied.
And you each gentle animal
  In confidence may bind,
And make them follow at your will,
  If you are only kind.

—From *McGuffey's Primer*

# THE NEW MOON

### Eliza Lee Follen

Dear mother, how pretty
The moon looks tonight!
She was never so cunning before:
Her two little horns
Are so sharp and so bright,
I hope she'll not grow any more.

If I were up there,
With you and my friends,
I'd rock in it nicely, you'd see;
I'd sit in the middle
And hold by both ends;
Oh, what a bright cradle 'twould be!

I would call to the stars
To keep out of the way,
Lest we should rock over their toes;
And then I would rock
Till the dawn of the day,
And see where the pretty moon goes.

And there we would stay
In the beautiful skies,
And through the bright clouds we would roam;
We would see the sun set,
And see the sun rise,
And in the next rainbow come home.

## THE PURPLE COW

Frank Gelett Burgess

I never Saw a Purple Cow;
    I never Hope to See One;
But I can Tell you, Anyhow,
    I'd rather See than Be One.

## A WISE OLD OWL

Edward Hersey Richards

A wise old owl sat on an oak,
The more he saw the less he spoke;
The less he spoke the more he heard;
Why aren't we like that wise old bird?

## THANKSGIVING DAY

Lydia Maria Child

Over the river and through the wood,
  To grandfather's house we go;
    The horse knows the way
    To carry the sleigh
  Through the white and drifted snow.

Over the river and through the wood—
  Oh, how the wind does blow!
    It stings the toes
    And bites the nose,
  As over the ground we go.

Over the river and through the wood,
  To have a first-rate play.
    Hear the bells ring,
    "Ting-a-ling-ding!"
  Hurrah for Thanksgiving Day!

Over the river and through the wood,
  Trot fast, my dapple gray!
    Spring over the ground,

Like a hunting hound!
For this is Thanksgiving Day.

Over the river and through the wood,
    And straight through the barnyard gate.
        We seem to go
        Extremely slow—
    It is so hard to wait!

Over the river and through the wood—
    Now grandmother's cap I spy!
        Hurrah for the fun!
        Is the pudding done?
    Hurrah for the pumpkin pie!


## THE YOUNG MYSTIC

Louis Untermeyer

We sat together close and warm,
    My little tired boy and I—
    Watching across the evening sky
The coming of the storm.

No rumblings rose, no thunder crashed,
    The west-wind scarcely sang aloud;
    But from a huge and solid cloud
The summer lightnings flashed.

Then he whispered, "Father, watch;
    I think God's going to light His moon—"
"And when, my boy . . ." "Oh, very soon.
I saw Him strike a match!"

## SEEIN' THINGS
### Eugene Field

I ain't afeard uv snakes, or toads, or bugs, or worms, or mice,
An' things 'at girls are skeered uv I think are awful nice!
I'm pretty brave, I guess; an' yet I hate to go to bed,
For, when I'm tucked up warm an' snug an' when my prayers are
    said,
Mother tells me, "Happy Dreams!" an' takes away the light,
An' leaves me lyin' all alone an' seein' things at night!

Sometimes they're in the corner, sometimes they're by the door,
Sometimes they're all a-standin' in the middle uv the floor;
Sometimes they are a-sittin' down, sometimes they're walkin' round
So softly and so creepy-like they never make a sound!
Sometimes they are as black as ink, an' other times they're white—
But the color ain't no difference when you see things at night!

Once, when I licked a feller 'at had just moved on our street,
An' father sent me up to bed without a bite to eat,
I woke up in the dark an' saw things standin' in a row,
A-lookin' at me cross-eyed an' p'intin' at me—so!
Oh, my! I wuz so skeered that time I never slep' a mite—
It's almost alluz when I'm bad I see things at night!

Lucky thing I ain't a girl, or I'd be skeered to death!
Bein' I'm a boy, I duck my head an' hold my breath;
An' I am, oh, *so* sorry I'm a naughty boy, an' then
I promise to be better an' I say my prayers again!
Gran'ma tells me that's the only way to make it right
When a feller has been wicked an' sees things at night!

An' so, when other naughty boys would coax me into sin,
I try to skwush the Tempter's voice 'at urges me within;
An' when they's pie for supper, or cakes 'at's big an' nice,
I want to—but I do not pass my plate f'r them things twice!
No, ruther let Starvation wipe me slowly out o' sight
Than I should keep a-livin' on an' seein' things at night!

## THE WIND AND THE LEAVES

George Cooper

"Come, little leaves," said the wind one day,
"Come o'er the meadows with me, and play;
Put on your dress of red and gold—
Summer is gone, and the days grow cold."

Soon as the leaves heard the wind's loud call,
Down they came fluttering, one and all;
Over the brown fields they danced and flew,
Singing the soft little songs they knew.

"Cricket, good-by, we've been friends so long;
Little brook, sing us your farewell song—

Say you are sorry to see us go;
Ah! you will miss us, right well we know.

"Dear little lambs, in your fleecy fold,
Mother will keep you from harm and cold;
Fondly we've watched you in vale and glade;
Say, will you dream of our loving shade?"

Dancing and whirling, the little leaves went;
Winter had called them, and they were content.
Soon fast asleep in their earthy beds,
The snow laid a coverlet over their heads.


## MERRY SUNSHINE

Anonymous

"Good-morning, Merry Sunshine,
    How did you wake so soon?
You've scared the little stars away
    And shined away the moon.
I saw you go to sleep last night
    Before I ceased my playing;
How did you get 'way over there?
    And where have you been staying?"

"I never go to sleep, dear child,
    I just go round to see
My little children of the east,
    Who rise and watch for me.
I waken all the birds and bees
    And flowers on my way,
And now come back to see the child
    Who stayed out late at play."

## THE SUGAR-PLUM TREE

Eugene Field

Have you ever heard of the Sugar-Plum Tree?
  'Tis a marvel of great renown!
It blooms on the shore of the Lollypop Sea
  In the garden of Shut-Eye Town;
The fruit that it bears is so wondrously sweet
  (As those who have tasted it say)
That good little children have only to eat
  Of that fruit to be happy next day.

When you've got to the tree, you would have a hard time
  To capture the fruit which I sing;
The tree is so tall that no person could climb
  To the boughs where the sugar-plums swing!
But up in that tree sits a chocolate cat,
  And a gingerbread dog prowls below—
And this is the way you contrive to get at
  Those sugar-plums tempting you so:

You say but the word to that gingerbread dog
  And he barks with such terrible zest
That the chocolate cat is at once all agog,
  As her swelling proportions attest.
And the chocolate cat goes cavorting around
  From this leafy limb unto that,

And the sugar-plums tumble, of course, to the ground—
    Hurrah for that chocolate cat!

There are marshmallows, gumdrops, and peppermint
      canes
    With stripings of scarlet and gold,
And you carry away of the treasure that rains
    As much as your apron can hold!
So come, little child, cuddle closer to me
    In your dainty white nightcap and gown,
And I'll rock you away to that Sugar-Plum Tree
    In the garden of Shut-Eye Town.

## THE THREE LITTLE KITTENS

Eliza Lee Follen

Three little kittens lost their mittens;
    And they began to cry,
     "Oh, mother dear,
      We very much fear
    That we have lost our mittens."
     "Lost your mittens!
     You naughty kittens!
    Then you shall have no pie!"
        "Mee-ow, mee-ow, mee-ow."
  "No, you shall have no pie."
        "Mee-ow, mee-ow, mee-ow."

The three little kittens found their mittens;
  And they began to cry,
  "Oh, mother dear,
    See here, see here!
See, we have found our mittens!"
  "Put on your mittens,
    You silly kittens,
And you may have some pie."
        "Purr-r, purr-r, purr-r,
Oh, let us have the pie!
        Purr-r, purr-r, purr-r."

The three little kittens put on their mittens,
  And soon ate up the pie;
  "Oh, mother dear,
    We greatly fear
That we have soiled our mittens!"
  "Soiled your mittens!
    You naughty kittens!"
Then they began to sigh,
        "Mee-ow, mee-ow, mee-ow."
Then they began to sigh,
        "Mee-ow, mee-ow, mee-ow."

The three little kittens washed their mittens,
  And hung them out to dry;
  "Oh, mother dear,
    Do not you hear
That we have washed our mittens?"
  "Washed your mittens!
    Oh, you're good kittens!
But I smell a rat close by,
        Hush, hush! Mee-ow, mee-ow."
"We smell a rat close by,
        Mee-ow, mee-ow, mee-ow."

## ROBERT OF LINCOLN

### William Cullen Bryant

Merrily swinging on brier and weed,
  Near to the nest of his little dame,
Over the mountainside or mead,
  Robert of Lincoln is telling his name:
   "Bob-o'-link, Bob-o'-link,
    Spink, spank, spink,
Snug and safe in that nest of ours,
Hidden among the summer flowers.
     Chee, chee, chee."

Robert of Lincoln is gayly drest,
  Wearing a bright black wedding-coat;
White are his shoulders and white is his crest.
  Hear him call in his merry note:
   "Bob-o'-link, Bob-o'-link,
    Spink, spank, spink;
Look, what a nice new coat is mine,
Sure there was never a bird so fine,
     Chee, chee, chee."

Robert of Lincoln's Quaker wife,
    Pretty and quiet, with plain brown wings,
Passing at home a patient life,
    Broods in the grass while her husband sings:
        "Bob-o'-link, Bob-o'-link,
            Spink, spank, spink;
Brood, kind creature; you need not fear
Thieves and robbers while I am here.
            Chee, chee, chee."

Modest and shy as a nun is she;
    One weak chirp is her only note.
Braggart and prince of braggarts is he,
    Pouring boasts from his little throat:
        "Bob-o'-link, Bob-o'-link,
            Spink, spank, spink;
Never was I afraid of man;
Catch me, cowardly knaves, if you can!
            Chee, chee, chee."

Six white eggs on a bed of hay,
    Flecked with purple, a pretty sight!
There as the mother sits all day,
    Robert is singing with all his might:
        "Bob-o'-link, Bob-o'-link,
            Spink, spank, spink;
Nice good wife, that never goes out,
Keeping house while I frolic about.
            Chee, chee, chee."

Soon as the little ones chip the shell,
    Six wide mouths are open for food;
Robert of Lincoln bestirs him well,
    Gathering seeds for the hungry brood.
        "Bob-o'-link, Bob-o'-link,

Spink, spank, spink;
This new life is likely to be
Hard for a gay young fellow like me.
    Chee, chee, chee."

Summer wanes; the children are grown;
    Fun and frolic no more he knows;
Robert of Lincoln's a humdrum crone;
    Off he flies, and we sing as he goes;
      Bob-o'-link, Bob-o'-link,
      Spink, spank, spink;
When you can pipe that merry old strain,
Robert of Lincoln, come back again.
    Chee, chee, chee.

## THE SANDMAN

Margaret Vandegrift (Margaret Thomson Janvier)

The rosy clouds float overhead,
    The sun is going down;
And now the sandman's gentle tread
    Comes stealing through the town.
"White sand, white sand," he softly cries,
    And as he shakes his hand,
Straightaway there lies on babies' eyes
    His gift of shining sand.
Blue eyes, gray eyes, black eyes, and brown,
    As shuts the rose, they softly close,
    When he goes through the town.

           —Selected from "The Sandman"

# THE RAILWAY TRAIN

### Emily Dickinson

I like to see it lap the miles,
And lick the valleys up,
And stop to feed itself at tanks;
And then, prodigious, step

Around a pile of mountains,
And, supercilious, peer
In shanties by the sides of roads;
And then a quarry pare

To fit its sides, and crawl between,
Complaining all the while
In horrid, hooting stanza;
Then chase itself down hill

And neigh like Boanerges;
Then, punctual as a star,
Stop—docile and omnipotent—
At its own stable door.

# LITTLE WILLIE

### Anonymous

Willie saw some dynamite,
Couldn't understand it quite;
Curiosity seldom pays:
It rained Willie seven days.

## WYNKEN, BLYNKEN, AND NOD

### A DUTCH LULLABY

Eugene Field

Wynken, Blynken, and Nod one night
   Sailed off in a wooden shoe—
Sailed on a river of crystal light
   Into a sea of dew.
"Where are you going, and what do you wish?"
   The old moon asked the three.
"We have come to fish for the herring fish
   That live in this beautiful sea;
   Nets of silver and gold have we!"
      Said Wynken,
      Blynken,
      And Nod.

The old moon laughed and sang a song,
   As they rocked in the wooden shoe;
And the wind that sped them all night long
   Ruffled the waves of dew.
The little stars were the herring fish
   That lived in that beautiful sea—
"Now cast your nets wherever you wish—
   Never afeared are we!"
   So cried the stars to the fishermen three,
      Wynken,
      Blynken,
      And Nod.

All night long their nets they threw
    To the stars in the twinkling foam—
Then down from the skies came the wooden shoe,
    Bringing the fishermen home;
'Twas all so pretty a sail it seemed
    As if it could not be,
And some folk thought 'twas a dream they'd dreamed
    Of sailing that beautiful sea—
    But I shall name you the fishermen three:
        Wynken,
        Blynken,
        And Nod.

Wynken and Blynken are two little eyes,
    And Nod is a little head,
And the wooden shoe that sailed the skies
    Is a wee one's trundle-bed;
So shut your eyes while Mother sings
    Of wonderful sights that be,
And you shall see the beautiful things
    As you rock in the misty sea
    Where the old shoe rocked the fishermen three:—
        Wynken,
        Blynken,
        And Nod.

# THE RUNAWAY

### Robert Frost

Once when the snow of the year was beginning to fall,
We stopped by a mountain pasture to say, 'Whose colt?'
A little Morgan had one forefoot on the wall,
The other curled at his breast. He dipped his head
And snorted to us. And then he had to bolt.
We heard the miniature thunder where he fled,
And we saw him, or thought we saw him, dim and gray,
Like a shadow against the curtain of falling flakes.

'I think the little fellow's afraid of the snow.
He isn't winter-broken. It isn't play
With the little fellow at all. He's running away.
I doubt if even his mother could tell him, "Sakes,
It's only weather." He'd think she didn't know!
Where is his mother? He can't be out alone.'
And now he comes again with clatter of stone,
And mounts the wall again with whited eyes
And all his tail that isn't hair up straight.
He shudders his coat as if to throw off flies.
'Whoever it is that leaves him out so late,
When other creatures have gone to stall and bin,
Ought to be told to come and take him in.'

## TRY, TRY AGAIN

### T. H. Palmer

'Tis a lesson you should heed,
   Try, try again;
If at first you don't succeed,
   Try, try again;
Then your courage should appear,
For, if you will persevere,
You will conquer, never fear;
   Try, try again.


## SUNSET

### Anonymous

Now the sun is sinking
   In the golden west;
Birds and bees and children
   All have gone to rest;
And the merry streamlet,
   As it runs along,
With a voice of sweetness
   Sings its evening song.

Cowslip, daisy, violet,
   In their little beds,
All among the grasses
   Hide their heavy heads;
There they'll all, sweet darlings,
   Lie in the happy dreams,
Till the rosy morning
   Wakes them with its beams.

—From *McGuffey's Third Reader*

# A VISIT FROM ST. NICHOLAS

Clement C. Moore

'Twas the night before Christmas, when all through the house
Not a creature was stirring, not even a mouse;
The stockings were hung by the chimney with care,
In hopes that St. Nicholas soon would be there.
The children were nestled all snug in their beds,
While visions of sugar-plums danced in their heads;
And mamma in her kerchief, and I in my cap,
Had just settled our brains for a long winter's nap;
When out on the lawn there arose such a clatter,
I sprang from the bed to see what was the matter.
Away to the window I flew like a flash,
Tore open the shutters and threw up the sash.
The moon on the breast of the new-fallen snow,
Gave the luster of midday to objects below,
When, what to my wondering eyes should appear,
But a miniature sleigh and eight tiny reindeer,
With a little old driver, so lively and quick,
I knew in a moment it must be St. Nick.
More rapid than eagles his coursers they came,
And he whistled, and shouted, and called them by name:
"Now, *Dasher!* now, *Dancer!* now, *Prancer* and *Vixen!*
On *Comet!* on, *Cupid!* on, *Donder* and *Blitzen!*
To the top of the porch, to the top of the wall!
Now, dash away! dash away! dash away all!"
As dry leaves that before the wild hurricane fly,
When they meet with an obstacle, mount to the sky,
So up to the house-top the coursers they flew,
With the sleigh full of toys, and St. Nicholas, too.
And then, in a twinkling, I heard on the roof

The prancing and pawing of each little hoof.
As I drew in my head, and was turning around,
Down the chimney St. Nicholas came with a bound.
He was dressed all in fur, from his head to his foot,
And his clothes were all tarnished with ashes and soot;
A bundle of toys he had flung on his back,
And he looked like a peddler just opening his pack.
His eyes—how they twinkled! his dimples how merry!
His cheeks were like roses, his nose like a cherry.
His droll little mouth was drawn up like a bow,
And the beard of his chin was as white as the snow.
The stump of a pipe he held tight in his teeth,
And the smoke it encircled his head like a wreath.
He had a broad face and a little round belly
That shook, when he laughed, like a bowlful of jelly.
He was chubby and plump, a right jolly old elf,
And I laughed when I saw him, in spite of myself.
A wink of his eye and a twist of his head
Soon gave me to know I had nothing to dread.
He spoke not a word, but went straight to his work,
And filled all the stockings; then turned with a jerk,
And laying his finger aside of his nose,
And giving a nod, up the chimney he rose.
He sprang to his sleigh, to his team gave a whistle,
And away they all flew like the down of a thistle.
But I heard him exclaim, ere he drove out of sight,
*"Happy Christmas to all, and to all a good-night!"*

# TEN LITTLE INJUNS

Anonymous

Ten little Injuns standing in a line—
One went home, and then there were nine.

Nine little Injuns swinging on a gate—
One tumbled off, and then there were eight.

Eight little Injuns tried to get to Heaven—
One kicked the bucket, and then there were seven.

Seven little Injuns cutting up tricks—
One went to bed, and then there were six.

Six little Injuns learning how to dive—
One swam away, and then there were five.

Five little Injuns on a cellar door—
One jumped off, and then there were four.

Four little Injuns climbing up a tree—
One fell down, and then there were three.

Three little Injuns out in a canoe—
One fell overboard, and then there were two.

Two little Injuns fooling with a gun—
One shot the other, and then there was one.

One little Injun living all alone—
He got married, and then there was none!

## THE GREEN GRASS GROWING
## ALL AROUND
### Anonymous

There was a tree stood in the ground,
The prettiest tree you ever did see;
The tree in the wood, and the wood in the ground,
And the green grass growing all around.
*And the green grass growing all around.*

And on this tree there was a limb,
The prettiest limb you ever did see;
The limb on the tree, and the tree in the wood,
The tree in the wood, and the wood in the ground,
And the green grass growing all around.
*And the green grass growing all around.*

[ 81 ]

And on this limb there was a bough,
The prettiest bough you ever did see;
The bough on the limb, and the limb on the tree,
The limb on the tree, and the tree in the wood,
The tree in the wood, and the wood in the ground,
And the green grass growing all around.
*And the green grass growing all around.*

Now on this bough there was a nest,
The prettiest nest you ever did see;
The nest on the bough, and the bough on the limb,
The bough on the limb, and the limb on the tree,
The limb on the tree, and the tree in the wood,
The tree in the wood, and the wood in the ground,
And the green grass growing all around.
*And the green grass growing all around.*

And in the nest there were some eggs,
The prettiest eggs you ever did see;
The eggs in the nest, and the nest on the bough,
The nest on the bough, and the bough on the limb,
The bough on the limb, and the limb on the tree,
The limb on the tree, and the tree in the wood,
The tree in the wood, and the wood in the ground,
And the green grass growing all around.
*And the green grass growing all around.*

# 2

# YOUTH

mister mckee

## ALADDIN

James Russell Lowell

When I was a beggarly boy,
    And lived in a cellar damp,
I had not a friend nor a toy,
    But I had Aladdin's lamp;
When I could not sleep for cold,
    I had fire enough in my brain,
And builded, with roofs of gold,
    My beautiful castles in Spain!

—Selected from "Aladdin"


## BIRD MUSIC

Donald Culross Peattie

The time to hear bird music is between four and six in the morning. Seven o'clock is not too late, but by eight the fine rapture is over, due, I suspect, to the contentment of the inner man that comes with breakfast; a poet should always be hungry or have a lost love.

—From *An Almanac for Moderns*

[ 85 ]

## APRIL RAIN

Robert Loveman

It is not raining rain for me,
   It's raining daffodils;
In every dimpled drop I see
   Wild flowers on the hills.

The clouds of gray engulf the day
   And overwhelm the town;
It is not raining rain to me,
   It's raining roses down.

It is not raining rain to me,
   But fields of clover bloom,
Where any buccaneering bee
   Can find a bed and room.

A health unto the happy,
   A fig for him who frets!
It is not raining rain to me,
   It's raining violets.

## DUTY

Ralph Waldo Emerson

So nigh is grandeur to our dust,
So near is God to man,
When Duty whispers low, "*Thou must,*"
The youth replies, "*I can.*"

—From "Voluntaries"

## A BOOK

### Emily Dickinson

He ate and drank the precious words,
His spirit grew robust;
He knew no more that he was poor,
Nor that his frame was dust.
He danced along the dingy days,
And this bequest of wings
Was but a book.  What liberty
A loosened spirit brings.

## AUTUMN

### Emily Dickinson

The morns are meeker than they were,
The nuts are getting brown;
The berry's cheek is plumper,
The rose is out of town.
The maple wears a gayer scarf,
The field a scarlet gown.
Lest I should be old-fashioned,
I'll put a trinket on.

## CASEY AT THE BAT

Ernest Lawrence Thayer

The outlook wasn't brilliant for the Mudville nine that day;
The score stood four to two with but one inning more to play.
And then when Cooney died at first and Barrows did the same,
A sickly silence fell upon the patrons of the game.

A struggling few got up to go in deep despair.  The rest
Clung to the hope which springs eternal in the human breast;
They thought if only Casey could but get a whack at that—
We'd put up even money now with Casey at the bat.

But Flynn preceded Casey, as did also Jimmy Blake,
And the former was a lulu and the latter was a cake;
So upon that stricken multitude grim melancholy sat,
For there seemed but little chance of Casey's getting to the bat.

But Flynn let drive a single, to the wonderment of all,
And Blake, the much despised, tore the cover off the ball;
And when the dust had lifted, and the men saw what had occurred,
There was Jimmy safe at second and Flynn a-hugging third.

Then from five thousand throats and more there rose a lusty yell;
It rumbled through the valley, it rattled in the dell;

It knocked upon the mountain and recoiled upon the flat,
For Casey, mighty Casey, was advancing to the bat.

There was ease in Casey's manner as he stepped into his place;
There was pride in Casey's bearing and a smile on Casey's face.
And when, responding to the cheers, he lightly doffed his hat,
No stranger in the crowd could doubt 'twas Casey at the bat.

Ten thousand eyes were on him as he rubbed his hands with dirt;
Five thousand tongues applauded when he wiped them on his shirt.
Then while the writhing pitcher ground the ball into his hip,
Defiance gleamed in Casey's eye, a sneer curled Casey's lip.

And now the leather-covered sphere came hurtling through the air,
And Casey stood a-watching it in haughty grandeur there.
Close by the sturdy batsman the ball unheeded sped—
"That ain't my style," said Casey. "Strike one," the umpire said.

From the benches, black with people, there went up a muffled roar,
Like the beating of the storm waves on a stern and distant shore.
"Kill him! Kill the umpire!" shouted someone on the stand;
And it's likely they'd have killed him had not Casey raised his hand.

With a smile of Christian charity great Casey's visage shone;
He stilled the rising tumult; he bade the game go on;
He signaled to the pitcher, and once more the spheroid flew;
But Casey still ignored it, and the umpire said, "Strike two."

"Fraud!" cried the maddened thousands, and echo answered,
        "Fraud!"
But one scornful look from Casey and the audience was awed.
They saw his face grow stern and cold, they saw his muscles strain,
And they knew that Casey wouldn't let that ball go by again.

The sneer is gone from Casey's lip, his teeth are clinched in hate;

He pounds with cruel violence his bat upon the plate.
And now the pitcher holds the ball, and now he lets it go,
And now the air is shattered by the force of Casey's blow.

Oh, somewhere in this favored land the sun is shining bright;
The band is playing somewhere, and somewhere hearts are light,
And somewhere men are laughing, and somewhere children shout;
But there is no joy in Mudville—mighty Casey has struck out.

—From the *San Francisco Examiner* of Sunday morning, June 3, 1888

## A BAKER'S DUZZEN UV WIZE SAWZ

Edward Rowland Sill

Them ez wants, must choose.
Them ez hez, must lose.
Them ez knows, won't blab.
Them ez guesses, will gab.
Them ez borrows, sorrows.
Them ez lends, spends.
Them ez gives, lives.
Them ez keeps dark, is deep.
Them ez kin earn, kin keep.
Them ez aims, hits.
Them ez hez, gits.
Them ez waits, wins.
Them ez *will, kin.*

[ 90 ]

# THE MODERN HIAWATHA

George A. Strong

He killed the noble Mudjokivis,
With the skin he made him mittens,
Made them with the fur side inside,
Made them with the skin side outside,
He, to get the warm side inside,
Put the inside skin side outside:
He, to get the cold side outside,
Put the warm side fur side inside:
That's why he put the fur side inside,
Why he put the skin side outside,
Why he turned them inside outside.

—From "The Song of Milkanwatha"


# BARTER

Sara Teasdale

Life has loveliness to sell,
    All beautiful and splendid things,
Blue waves whitened on a cliff,
    Soaring fire that sways and sings,
And children's faces looking up
Holding wonder like a cup.

Life has loveliness to sell,
    Music like a curve of gold,
Scent of pine trees in the rain,
    Eyes that love you, arms that hold,
And for your spirit's still delight,
Holy thoughts that star the night.

—Selected from "Barter"

[ 91 ]

# NONSENSE JINGLES

Anonymous

Mother may I go out to swim?
Yes, my darling daughter.
Hang your clothes on a hickory limb,
But don't go near the water.

\* \* \*

Sam, Sam, the butcher man,
Washed his face in a frying pan,
Combed his hair with a wagon wheel,
And died of a toothache in his heel.

\* \* \*

Fishy, fishy in the brook,
Daddy catch him with a hook,
Mama fry him in a pan,
Baby eat him like a man.

\* \* \*

I asked my mother for fifty cents
To see the elephant jump the fence.
He jumped so high he touched the sky
And never came down till the Fourth of July.

\* \* \*

Adam and Eve and Pinch-me
Went down to the river to bathe.
Adam and Eve were drown-ded.
Who do you think was saved?

\* \* \*

One for the money, two for the show,
Three to get ready, and four to go.

Hippity-hop to the barber shop
To get a stick of candy.
One for you and one for me
And one for sister Sandy.

\* \* \*

Star light, star bright,
First star I see tonight,
I wish I may, I wish I might
Have the wish I wish tonight.

\* \* \*

Open your mouth and shut your eyes,
And I'll give you something to make you wise.

\* \* \*

I like coffee, I like tea,
I like girls, and girls like me.

\* \* \*

Two's company, three's a crowd,
Four on the sidewalk is not allowed.

## FOR OF ALL SAD WORDS

John Greenleaf Whittier

For of all sad words of tongue or pen,
The saddest are these: "It might have been!"

—From "Maud Muller"

## EN VOYAGE
Caroline Atwater Mason

Whichever way the wind doth blow,
Some heart is glad to have it so;
Then blow it east or blow it west,
The wind that blows, that wind is best.

My little craft sails not alone;
A thousand fleets from every zone
Are out upon a thousand seas;
And what for me were favoring breeze
Might dash another, with the shock
Of doom, upon some hidden rock.
And so I do not dare to pray
For winds to waft me on my way,
But leave it to a Higher Will
To stay or speed me; trusting still
That all is well, and sure that He
Who launched my bark will sail with me
Through storm and calm, and will not fail,
Whatever breezes may prevail,
To land me, every peril past,
Within His sheltering haven at last.

Then, whatsoever wind doth blow,
My heart is glad to have it so;
And blow it east or blow it west,
The wind that blows, that wind is best.

## ETERNAL PARTNERSHIP

### Edwin Arlington Robinson

Look at a branch, a bird, a child, a rose,
Or anything God ever made that grows—
Nor let the smallest vision of it slip,
Till you may read, as on Belshazzar's wall,
The glory of eternal partnership.


## FOR CHRISTMAS

### Rachel Field

Now not a window small or big
But wears a wreath of holly sprig;
Nor any shop too poor to show
Its spray of pine or mistletoe.
Now city airs are spicy-sweet
With Christmas trees along each street,
Green spruce and fir whose boughs will hold
Their tinselled balls and fruits of gold.
Now postmen pass in threes and fours
Like bent, blue-coated Santa Claus.
Now people hurry to and fro
With little girls and boys in tow,
And not a child but keeps some trace
Of Christmas secrets in his face.

## THE DAY IS DONE

Henry Wadsworth Longfellow

The day is done, and the darkness
  Falls from the wings of Night,
As a feather is wafted downward
  From an eagle in his flight.

I see the lights of the village
  Gleam through the rain and the mist,
And a feeling of sadness comes o'er me
  That my soul cannot resist:

A feeling of sadness and longing,
  That is not akin to pain,
And resembles sorrow only
  As the mist resembles the rain.

Come, read to me some poem,
  Some simple and heartfelt lay,
That shall soothe this restless feeling,
  And banish the thoughts of day.

Not from the grand old masters,
  Not from the bards sublime,
Whose distant footsteps echo
  Through the corridors of Time.

For, like strains of martial music,
　　Their mighty thoughts suggest
Life's endless toil and endeavor;
　　And tonight I long for rest.

Read from some humbler poet,
　　Whose songs gushed from his heart,
As showers from the clouds of summer,
　　Or tears from the eyelids start;

Who, through long days of labor,
　　And nights devoid of ease,
Still heard in his soul the music
　　Of wonderful melodies.

Such songs have power to quiet
　　The restless pulse of care,
And come like the benediction
　　That follows after prayer.

Then read from the treasured volume
　　The poem of thy choice,
And lend to the rhyme of the poet
　　The beauty of thy voice.

And the night shall be filled with music
　　And the cares that infest the day,
Shall fold their tents, like the Arabs,
　　And as silently steal away.

# THE FIRST SNOW-FALL

James Russell Lowell

The snow had begun in the gloaming,
    And busily all the night
Had been heaping field and highway
    With a silence deep and white.

Every pine and fir and hemlock
    Wore ermine too dear for an earl,
And the poorest twig on the elm-tree
    Was ridged inch deep with pearl.

From sheds new-roofed with Carrara
    Came Chanticleer's muffled crow,
The stiff rails softened to swan's-down,
    And still fluttered down the snow.

I stood and watched by the window
    The noiseless work of the sky,
And the sudden flurries of snow-birds,
    Like brown leaves whirling by.

—Selected from "The First Snow-Fall"


# FOG

Carl Sandburg

The fog comes
on little cat feet.
It sits looking
over harbor and city
on silent haunches
and then moves on.

[ 98 ]

## THE BELLS

### Edgar Allan Poe

Hear the sledges with the bells—
    Silver bells!
What a world of merriment their melody foretells!
    How they tinkle, tinkle, tinkle,
      In the icy air of night!
    While the stars that oversprinkle
    All the heavens seem to twinkle
      With a crystalline delight;
    Keeping time, time, time,
    In a sort of Runic rhyme,
To the tintinnabulation that so musically wells
    From the bells, bells, bells, bells,
        Bells, bells, bells—
From the jingling and the tinkling of the bells.

—Selected from "The Bells"

# EULOGY OF THE DOG

George G. Vest

Gentlemen of the Jury: The best friend a man has in the world may turn against him and become his enemy. His son or daughter whom he has reared with loving care may prove ungrateful. Those who are nearest and dearest to us, those whom we trust with our happiness and our good name, may become traitors to their faith. The money that a man has he may lose. It flies away from him, perhaps when he needs it most. A man's reputation may be sacrificed in a moment of ill-considered action. The people who are prone to fall on their knees to do us honor when success is with us may be the first to throw the stone of malice when failure settles its clouds upon our heads.

The one absolutely unselfish friend that man can have in this selfish world, the one that never deserts him, the one that never proves ungrateful or treacherous, is his dog. A man's dog stands by him in prosperity and in poverty, in health and in sickness. He will sleep on the cold ground, where the wintry winds blow and the snow drives fiercely, if only he can be near his master's side. He will kiss the hand that has no food to offer, he will lick the wounds and sores that come in encounter with the roughness of the world. He guards the sleep of his pauper master as if he were a prince. When all other friends desert, he remains. When riches take wings and reputation falls to pieces, he is as constant in his love as the sun in its journey through the heavens.

If fortune drives the master forth an outcast in the world, friendless and homeless, the faithful dog asks no higher privilege than that of accompanying him, to guard against danger, to fight against his enemies. And when the last scene of all comes, and death takes his master in its embrace, and his body is laid away in the cold ground, no matter if all other friends pursue their way, there by the graveside will the noble dog be found, his head between his paws, his eyes sad but open in alert watchfulness, faithful and true even to death.

## FATHER'S EDUCATION
### Mark Twain (Samuel L. Clemens)

When I was a boy of fourteen, my father was so ignorant I could hardly stand to have the old man around. But when I got to be twenty-one, I was astonished at how much the old man had learned in seven years.

## FER A DOG
### Edward Noyes Westcott

They say a reasonable amount o' fleas is good fer a dog—keeps him from broodin' over *bein'* a dog, mebbe.

—From *David Harum*

## HOW TO TELL BAD NEWS

Anonymous

(*Mr. H. and the Steward talking*)

*Mr. H.*   Ha! Steward, how are you, my old boy?  How do things go on at home?

*Steward.*   Bad enough, your honor; the magpie's dead.

*H.*   Poor Mag! So he's gone. How came he to die?

*S.*   Overeat himself, sir.

*H.*   Did he?  A greedy dog; why, what did he get he liked so well?

*S.*   Horseflesh, sir; he died of eating horseflesh.

*H.*   How came he to get so much horseflesh?

*S.*   All your father's horses, sir.

*H.*   What! are they dead, too?

*S.*   Aye, sir; they died of overwork.

*H.*   And why were they overworked, pray?

*S.*   To carry water, sir.

*H.*   To carry water! And what were they carrying water for?

*S.*   Sure, sir, to put out out the fire.

*H.*   Fire! what fire?

*S.*   Oh, sir, your father's house is burned to the ground.

*H.*   My father's house burned down! And how came it set on fire?

*S.*   I think, sir, it must have been the torches.

*H.*   Torches! what torches?

*S.*   At your mother's funeral.

*H.*  My mother dead!

*S.*  Ah, poor lady! She never looked up, after it.

*H.*  After what?

*S.*  The loss of your father.

*H.*  My father gone, too?

*S.*  Yes, poor gentleman! he took to his bed as soon as he heard of it.

*H.*  Heard of what?

*S.*  The bad news, sir, and please your honor.

*H.*  What! more miseries! more bad news!

*S.*  Yes, sir; your bank failed, and your credit is lost, and you are not worth a shilling in the world. I made bold, sir, to wait on you about it, for I thought you would like to hear the news.

—From *McGuffey's Fifth Reader*

## FORBEARANCE

### Ralph Waldo Emerson

Hast thou named all the birds without a gun?
Loved the wood-rose, and left it on its stalk?
At rich men's tables eaten bread and pulse?
Unarmed, faced danger with a heart of trust?
And loved so well a high behavior,
In man or maid, that thou from speech refrained,
Nobility more nobly to repay?
Oh, be my friend, and teach me to be thine!

# THE HEIGHT OF THE RIDICULOUS

Oliver Wendell Holmes

I wrote some lines once on a time
   In wondrous merry mood,
And thought, as usual, men would say
   They were exceeding good.

They were so queer, so very queer,
   I laughed as I would die;
Albeit, in the general way,
   A sober man am I.

I called my servant, and he came;
   How kind it was of him,
To mind a slender man like me,
   He of the mighty limb.

"These to the printer," I exclaimed,
   And in my humorous way,
I added (as a trifling jest),
   "There'll be the devil to pay."

He took the paper, and I watched,
   And saw him peep within;
At the first line he read, his face
   Was all upon the grin.

He read the next; the grin grew broad,
   And shot from ear to ear;
He read the third; a chuckling noise
   I now began to hear.

The fourth; he broke into a roar;
   The fifth; his waistband split;

The sixth; he burst five buttons off,
  And tumbled in a fit.

Ten days and nights, with sleepless eye,
  I watched that wretched man,
And since, I never dare to write
  As funny as I can.

## THE MELANCHOLY DAYS

### William Cullen Bryant

The melancholy days are come,
    the saddest of the year,
Of wailing winds, and naked woods,
    and meadows brown and sere;
Heaped in the hollows of the grove,
    the autumn leaves lie dead;
They rustle to the eddying gust,
    and to the rabbit's tread;
The robin and the wren are flown,
    and from the shrubs the jay,
And from the wood-top calls the crow
    through all the gloomy day.

    —From "The Death of the Flowers"

[ 105 ]

## JUNE

### James Russell Lowell

And what is so rare as a day in June?
   Then, if ever, come perfect days;
Then Heaven tries earth if it be in tune,
   And over it softly her warm ear lays;
Whether we look, or whether we listen,
   We hear life murmur, or see it glisten;

Every clod feels a stir of might,
   An instinct within it that reaches and towers,
And, groping blindly above it for light,
   Climbs to a soul in grass and flowers;
The flush of life may well be seen
   Thrilling back over hills and valleys;
The cowslip startles in meadow green,
   The buttercup catches the sun in its chalice,
And there's never a leaf nor a blade too mean
   To be some happy creature's palace;
The little bird sits at his door in the sun,
   Atilt like a blossom among the leaves,
And lets his illumined being o'errun
   With the deluge of summer it receives;
His mate feels the eggs beneath her wings,
And the heart in her dumb breast flutters and sings;

[ 106 ]

He sings to the wide world, and she to her nest—
In the nice ear of Nature which song is the best?

Now is the high-tide of the year,
   And whatever of life hath ebbed away
Comes flooding back with a ripply cheer,
   Into every bare inlet and creek and bay;
Now the heart is so full that a drop over-fills it,
We are happy now because God wills it;
No matter how barren the past may have been,
Tis enough for us now that the leaves are green;
We sit in the warm shade and feel right well
How the sap creeps up and the blossoms swell;
We may shut our eyes, but we cannot help knowing
That skies are clear and grass is growing;
The breeze comes whispering in our ear,
That dandelions are blossoming near,
   That maize has sprouted, that streams are flowing,
That the river is bluer than the sky,
That the robin is plastering his house hard by;
And if the breeze kept the good news back,
For other couriers we should not lack;
   We could guess it all by yon heifer's lowing—
And hark! how clear bold chanticleer,
Warmed with the new wine of the year,
   Tells all in his lusty crowing!

Joy comes, grief goes, we know not how;
Everything is happy now,
   Everything is upward striving;
'Tis as easy now for the heart to be true
As for grass to be green or skies to be blue—
   'Tis the natural way of living:
Who knows whither the clouds have fled?
   In the unscarred heaven they leave no wake;

And the eyes forget the tears they have shed,
  The heart forgets its sorrow and ache;
The soul partakes the season's youth,
  And the sulphurous rifts of passion and woe
Lie deep 'neath a silence pure and smooth,
  Like burnt-out craters healed with snow.

—From the Prelude to "The Vision of Sir Launfal"

## THE ARROW AND THE SONG

### Henry Wadsworth Longfellow

I shot an arrow into the air,
It fell to earth, I knew not where;
For, so swiftly it flew, the sight
Could not follow it in its flight.

I breathed a song into the air,
It fell to earth, I knew not where;
For who has sight so keen and strong
That it can follow the flight of song?

Long, long afterward, in an oak
I found the arrow, still unbroke;
And the song, from beginning to end,
I found again in the heart of a friend.

## JINGLE BELLS

### John Pierpont

Dashing thro' the snow in a one-horse open sleigh,
O'er the fields we go, laughing all the way;
Bells on bob-tail ring, making spirits bright;
What fun it is to ride and sing a sleighing song tonight!

*Chorus:*
Jingle bells! Jingle bells! Jingle all the way!
Oh! what fun it is to ride in a one-horse open sleigh!

A day or two ago I thought I'd take a ride,
And soon Miss Fanny Bright was seated by my side;
The horse was lean and lank, misfortune seemed his lot,
He got into a drifted bank, and we, we got upsot.

Now the ground is white, go it while you're young,
Take the girls tonight, and sing this sleighing song;
Just get a bob-tailed nag, two-forty for his speed,
Then hitch him to an open sleigh, and crack! you'll take
    the lead.

# LIMERICKS

There was an old man of Nantucket
Who kept all his cash in a bucket;
    But his daughter, named Nan,
    Ran away with a man—
And as for the bucket, Nantucket.

                         —Anonymous

         \*   \*   \*

She frowned and called him Mr.
Because in sport he kr.
    And so in spite
    That very night
This Mr. kr. sr.

                         —Anonymous

         \*   \*   \*

A fly and a flea in a flue
Were imprisoned, so what could they do?
    Said the fly, "Let us flee,"
    Said the flea, "Let us fly,"
So they flew through a flaw in the flue.

                         —Anonymous

         \*   \*   \*

As a beauty I am not a star,
There are others more handsome, by far,
    But my face—I don't mind it,
    Because I'm behind it,
'Tis the folks in the front that I jar.

—A favorite limerick of Woodrow Wilson, by Anthony Euwer

# HOME, SWEET HOME
### John Howard Payne

'Mid pleasures and palaces though we may roam,
Be it ever so humble, there's no place like home;
A charm from the sky seems to hallow us there,
Which, seek through the world, is ne'er met with elsewhere.
Home, home, sweet, sweet home!
There's no place like home! There's no place like home!

An exile from home, splendor dazzles in vain;
Oh, give me my lowly thatched cottage again!
The birds singing gayly, that came at my call—
Give me them—and the peace of mind, dearer than all!
Home, home, sweet, sweet home!
There's no place like home! There's no place like home!

How sweet 'tis to sit 'neath a fond father's smile,
And the caress of a mother to soothe and beguile!
Let others delight mid new pleasures to roam,
But give me, oh, give me, the pleasures of home!
Home, home, sweet, sweet home!
There's no place like home! There's no place like home!

To thee I'll return, overburdened with care;
The heart's dearest solace will smile on me there;
No more from that cottage again will I roam;
Be it ever so humble, there's no place like home.
Home, home, sweet, sweet home!
There's no place like home! There's no place like home!

## A LITTLE WORD

### Daniel Clement Colesworthy

A little word in kindness spoken,
    A motion or a tear,
Has often healed the heart that's broken,
    And made a friend sincere.

—Selected from "A Little Word"

## THE LADDER

### Josiah Gilbert Holland

Heaven is not reached at a single bound;
    But we build the ladder by which we rise
    From the lowly earth to the vaulted skies,
And we mount to its summit round by round.

—From "Gradatim"

## NOW

Charles R. Skinner

If you have hard work to do,
    Do it now.
Today the skies are clear and blue,
Tomorrow clouds may come in view,
Yesterday is not for you;
    Do it now.

If you have a song to sing,
    Sing it now.
Let the notes of gladness ring
Clear as song of bird in Spring,
Let every day some music bring;
    Sing it now.

If you have kind words to say,
    Say them now.
Tomorrow may not come your way,
Do a kindness while you may,
Loved ones will not always stay;
    Say them now.

If you have a smile to show,
    Show it now.
Make hearts happy, roses grow,
Let the friends around you know
The love you have before they go;
    Show it now.

## IN SCHOOL-DAYS

John Greenleaf Whittier

Still sits the schoolhouse by the road,
  A ragged beggar sleeping;
Around it still the sumachs grow,
  And blackberry-vines are creeping.

Within, the master's desk is seen,
  Deep scarred by raps official;
The warping floor, the battered seats,
  The jackknife's carved initial;

The charcoal frescoes on its wall;
  Its door's worn sill, betraying
The feet that, creeping slow to school,
  Went storming out to playing!

Long years ago a winter sun
  Shone over it at setting;
Lit up its western windowpanes,
  And low eaves' icy fretting.

It touched the tangled golden curls,
  And brown eyes full of grieving,
Of one who still her steps delayed
  When all the school were leaving.

For near her stood the little boy
  Her childish favor singled:
His cap pulled low upon a face
  Where pride and shame were mingled.

Pushing with restless feet the snow
  To right and left, he lingered;—
As restlessly her tiny hands
  The blue-checked apron fingered.

He saw her lift her eyes; he felt
  The soft hand's light caressing,
And heard the tremble of her voice,
  As if a fault confessing.

"I'm sorry that I spelt the word:
  I hate to go above you,
Because"—the brown eyes lower fell—
  "Because, you see, I love you!"

—Selected from "In School-days"

## LOOK UP

### Edward Everett Hale

To Look up and not down,
To Look forward and not back,
To Look out and not in, and
To Lend a hand.

—From "Ten Times One Is Ten"

# THE OLD SWIMMIN'-HOLE

### James Whitcomb Riley

Oh! the old swimmin'-hole! whare the crick so still and deep
Looked like a baby-river that was laying half asleep,
And the gurgle of the worter round the drift jest below
Sounded like the laugh of something we onc't ust to know
Before we could remember anything but the eyes
Of the angels lookin' out as we left Paradise;
But the merry days of youth is beyond our controle,
And it's hard to part ferever with the old swimmin'-hole.

Oh! the old swimmin'-hole! In the happy days of yore,
When I ust to lean above it on the old sickamore,
Oh! it showed me a face in its warm sunny tide
That gazed back at me so gay and glorified,
It made me love myself, as I leaped to caress
My shadder smilin' up at me with sich tenderness.
But them days is past and gone, and old Time's tuck his toll
From the old man come back to the old swimmin'-hole.

Oh! the old swimmin'-hole! In the long, lazy days
When the humdrum of school made so many run-a-ways,
How pleasant was the jurney down the old dusty lane,
Whare the tracks of our bare feet was all printed so plane
You could tell by the dent of the heel and the sole
They was lots o' fun on hand at the old swimmin'-hole.
But the lost joys is past! Let your tears in sorrow roll
Like the rain that ust to dapple up the old swimmin'-hole.

Thare the bulrushes growed, and the cattails so tall,
And the sunshine and shadder fell over it all;
And it mottled the worter with amber and gold
Tel the glad lilies rocked in the ripples that rolled;
And the snake-feeder's four gauzy wings fluttered by
Like the ghost of a daisy dropped out of the sky,
Or a wounded apple-blossom in the breeze's controle
As it cut acrost some orchard to'rds the old swimmin'-hole.

Oh! the old swimmin'-hole! When I last saw the place,
The scenes was all changed, like the change in my face;
The bridge of the railroad now crosses the spot
Whare the old divin'-log lays sunk and fergot.
And I stray down the banks whare the trees ust to be—
But never again will theyr shade shelter me!
And I wish in my sorrow I could strip to the soul,
And dive off in my grave like the old swimmin'-hole.

# OCTOBER'S BRIGHT BLUE WEATHER

Helen Hunt Jackson

O sun and skies and clouds of June,
   And flowers of June together,
Ye cannot rival for one hour
   October's bright blue weather,

When loud the bumblebee makes haste,
   Belated, thriftless vagrant,
And goldenrod is dying fast,
   And lanes with grapes are fragrant;

When gentians roll their fingers tight
   To save them for the morning,
And chestnuts fall from satin burrs
   Without a sound of warning;

When on the ground red apples lie
   In piles like jewels shining,
And redder still on old stone walls
   Are leaves of woodbine twining;

When all the lovely wayside things
   Their white-winged seeds are sowing,
And in the fields, still green and fair,
   Late aftermaths are growing;

When springs run low, and on the brooks,
   In idle golden freighting,
Bright leaves sink noiseless in the hush
   Of woods, for winter waiting;

When comrades seek sweet country haunts,
   By twos and twos together,

And count like misers, hour by hour,
  October's bright blue weather.

O sun and skies and flowers of June,
  Count all your boasts together,
Love loveth best of all the year
  October's bright blue weather.

## THE PERT CHICKEN

Marian Douglas

There was once a pretty chicken;
  But his friends were very few,
For he thought that there was nothing
  In the world but what he knew:
So he always, in the farmyard,
  Had a very forward way,
Telling all the hens and turkeys
  What they ought to do and say.
"Mrs. Goose," he said, "I wonder
  That your goslings you should let
Go out paddling in the water;
  It will kill them to get wet."

"I wish, my old Aunt Dorking,"
  He began to her, one day,
"That you wouldn't sit all summer
  In your nest upon the hay.
Won't you come out to the meadow,

Where the grass with seeds is filled?"
"If I should," said Mrs. Dorking,
  "Then my eggs would all get chilled."
"No, they won't," replied the chicken,
  "And no matter if they do;
Eggs are really good for nothing;
  What's an egg to me or you?"

"What's an egg!" said Mrs. Dorking,
  "Can it be you do not know
You yourself were in an eggshell
  Just one little month ago?
And, if kind wings had not warmed you,
  You would not be out today,
Telling hens, and geese, and turkeys,
  What they ought to do and say!
To be very wise, and show it,
  Is a pleasant thing, no doubt;
But, when young folks talk to old folks,
  They should know what they're about."

—From *McGuffey's Third Reader*

## *On* DIGITAL EXTREMITIES

### Gelett Burgess

I'd Rather have Fingers than Toes;
I'd Rather have Eyes than a Nose;
  And As for my hair,
  I'm Glad it's all there;
I'll be Awfully Sad, when it Goes!

# HOME
### Edgar A. Guest

It takes a heap o' livin' in a house t' make it home,
A heap o' sun an' shadder, an' ye sometimes have t' roam
Afore ye really 'preciate the things ye lef' behind,
An' hunger fer 'em somehow, with 'em allus on yer mind.
It don't make any differunce how rich ye get t' be,
How much yer chairs an' tables cost, how great yer luxury;
It ain't home t' ye, though it be the palace of a king,
Until somehow yer soul is sort o' wrapped round everything.

Home ain't a place that gold can buy or get up in a minute;
Afore it's home there's got t' be a heap o' livin' in it;
Within the walls there's got t' be some babies born, and then
Right there ye've got t' bring 'em up t' women good, an' men;
And gradjerly, as time goes on, ye find ye wouldn't part
With anything they ever used—they've grown into yer heart:
The old high chairs, the playthings, too, the little shoes they wore
Ye hoard; an' if ye could ye'd keep the thumb-marks on the door.

—Selected from "Home"

## PRIMER LESSON

### Carl Sandburg

Look out how you use proud words.
When you let proud words go, it is not
    easy to call them back.
They wear long boots, hard boots;
    they walk off proud; they can't
    hear you calling—
Look out how you use proud words.


## LEND A HAND

### Anonymous

Lend a hand to one another
In the daily toil of life;
When we meet a weaker brother,
Let us help him in the strife.
There is none so rich but may,
In his turn, be forced to borrow;
And the poor man's lot today
May become our own tomorrow.

## THE FOREST PRIMEVAL
### Henry Wadsworth Longfellow

This is the forest primeval. The murmuring pines and the hemlocks,
Bearded with moss, and in garments green, indistinct in the twilight,
Stand like Druids of eld, with voices sad and prophetic,
Stand like harpers hoar, with beards that rest on their bosoms.
Loud from its rocky caverns, the deep-voiced neighboring ocean
Speaks, and in accents disconsolate answers the wail of the forest.

*—From the Prelude to "Evangeline"*

## THE PASTURE
### Robert Frost

I'm going out to clean the pasture spring;
I'll only stop to rake the leaves away
(And wait to watch the water clear, I may):
I sha'n't be gone long.—You come too.

I'm going out to fetch the little calf
That's standing by the mother. It's so young
It totters when she licks it with her tongue.
I sha'n't be gone long.—*You come too.*

[ 123 ]

## OUT TO OLD AUNT MARY'S

James Whitcomb Riley

Wasn't it pleasant, O brother mine,
In those old days of the lost sunshine
 Of youth—when the Saturday's chores were through
 And the "Sunday's wood" in the kitchen, too,
 And we went visiting, "me and you,"
  Out to Old Aunt Mary's?—

It all comes back so clear today!
Though I am as bald as you are gray,—
 Out by the barn-lot and down the lane
 We patter along in the dust again,
 As light as the tips of the drops of the rain,
  Out to Old Aunt Mary's.—

We cross the pasture, and through the wood,
Where the old gray snag of the poplar stood,
 Where the hammering "red-heads" hopped awry,
 And the buzzard "raised" in the "clearing"-sky
 And lolled and circled, as we went by
  Out to Old Aunt Mary's.—

And then in the dust of the road again;
And the teams we met, and the countrymen;
 And the long highway, with sunshine spread

As thick as butter on country bread,
Our cares behind, and our hearts ahead
　　Out to Old Aunt Mary's.—

Why, I see her now in the open door
Where the little gourds grew up the sides and o'er
　　The clapboard roof!—And her face—ah, me!
　　Wasn't it good for a boy to see—
　　And wasn't it good for a boy to be
　　　　Out to Old Aunt Mary's?—

For, O my brother so far away,
This is to tell you—she waits *today*
　　To welcome us:—Aunt Mary fell
　　Asleep this morning, whispering, "Tell
　　The boys to come" . . . And all is well
　　　　Out to Old Aunt Mary's.

　　　　　　　　—Selected from "Out to Old Aunt Mary's"

## ROCK ME TO SLEEP

Elizabeth Akers Allen

Backward, turn backward, O Time, in your flight,
Make me a child again, just for tonight!
Mother, come back from the echoless shore,
Take me again to your heart as of yore;
Kiss from my forehead the furrows of care,
Smooth the few silver threads out of my hair;
Over my slumbers your loving watch keep;—
Rock me to sleep, Mother—rock me to sleep!

　　　　　　　　—Selected from "Rock Me to Sleep"

## SNOW-BOUND

### John Greenleaf Whittier

The sun that brief December day
Rose cheerless over hills of gray,
And, darkly circled, gave at noon
A sadder light than waning moon.
Slow tracing down the thickening sky
Its mute and ominous prophecy,
A portent seeming less than threat,
It sank from sight before it set.
A chill no coat, however stout,
Of homespun stuff could quite shut out,
A hard, dull bitterness of cold,
That checked, mid-vein, the circling race
Of life-blood in the sharpened face,
The coming of the snow-storm told.
The wind blew east; we heard the roar
Of Ocean on his wintry shore,
And felt the strong pulse throbbing there
Beat with low rythm our inland air.

Meanwhile we did our nightly chores—
Brought in the wood from out of doors,

Littered the stalls, and from the mows
Raked down the herd's-grass for the cows:
Heard the horse whinnying for his corn;
And, sharply clashing horn on horn,
Impatient down the stanchion rows
The cattle shake their walnut brows;
While, peering from his early perch
Upon the scaffold's pole of birch,
The cock his crested helmet bent
And down his querulous challenge sent.

Unwarmed by any sunset light
The gray day darkened into night,
A night made hoary with the swarm
And whirl-dance of the blinding storm,
As zigzag, wavering to and fro,
Crossed and recrossed the winged snow:
And ere the early bedtime came
The white drift piled the window-frame,
And through the glass the clothesline posts
Looked in like tall and sheeted ghosts.
So all night long the storm roared on:
The morning broke without a sun;
In tiny spherule traced with lines
Of Nature's geometric signs,
In starry flake, and pellicle,
All day the hoary meteor fell;
And, when the second morning shone,
We looked upon a world unknown,
On nothing we could call our own.
Around the glistening wonder bent
The blue walls of the firmament,
No cloud above, no earth below—
A universe of sky and snow!
The old familiar sights of ours

Took marvelous shapes; strange domes and towers
Rose up where sty or corn-crib stood,
Or garden-wall, or belt of wood;
A smooth white mound the brush-pile showed,
A fenceless drift that once was road;
The bridle-post an old man sat
With loose-flung coat and high cocked hat;
The well-curb had a Chinese roof;
And even the long sweep, high aloof,
In its slant splendor, seemed to tell
Of Pisa's leaning miracle.

—Selected from "Snow-bound, A Winter Idyl"

## OUR LIPS AND EARS

Anonymous

If you your lips would keep from slips,
Five things observe with care:
Of whom you speak, to whom you speak,
And how and when and where.

If you your ears would save from jeers,
These things keep mildly hid:
"Myself" and "I," and "mine" and "my,"
And how "I" do and did.

## SOLITUDE

### Ella Wheeler Wilcox

Laugh, and the world laughs with you;
  Weep, and you weep alone;
For the sad old earth must borrow its mirth,
  But has trouble enough of its own.
Sing, and the hills will answer;
  Sigh, it is lost on the air.
The echoes bound to a joyful sound,
  But shrink from voicing care.

—Selected from "Solitude"

## SPEAK GENTLY

### David Bates

Speak gently; it is better far
  To rule by love than fear.
Speak gently; let no harsh word mar
  The good we may do here.

—Selected from "Speak Gently"

# OPPORTUNITY

### Berton Braley

With doubt and dismay you are smitten,
  You think there's no chance for you, son?
Why, the best books haven't been written,
  The best race hasn't been run.

—Selected from "Opportunity"

# THE RAINY DAY

### Henry Wadsworth Longfellow

The day is cold, and dark, and dreary;
It rains, and the wind is never weary;
The vine still clings to the mouldering wall,
But at every gust the dead leaves fall,
  And the day is dark and dreary.

My life is cold, and dark, and dreary;
It rains, and the wind is never weary;
My thoughts still cling to the mouldering Past,
But the hopes of youth fall thick in the blast,
  And the days are dark and dreary.

Be still, sad heart! and cease repining;
Behind the clouds is the sun still shining;
Thy fate is the common fate of all,
Into each life some rain must fall,
  Some days must be dark and dreary.

## A PSALM OF LIFE

Henry Wadsworth Longfellow

Tell me not, in mournful numbers,
　Life is but an empty dream!—
For the soul is dead that slumbers,
　And things are not what they seem.

Life is real! Life is earnest!
　And the grave is not its goal;
Dust thou art, to dust returnest,
　Was not spoken of the soul.

Not enjoyment, and not sorrow,
　Is our destined end or way;
But to act, that each tomorrow
　Find us farther than today.

Art is long, and Time is fleeting,
　And our hearts, though stout and brave,
Still, like muffled drums, are beating
　Funeral marches to the grave.

In the world's broad field of battle,
　In the bivouac of Life,
Be not like dumb, driven cattle!
　Be a hero in the strife!

Trust no Future, howe'er pleasant!
　　Let the dead Past bury its dead!
Act—act in the living Present!
　　Heart within, and God o'erhead!

Lives of great men all remind us
　　We can make our lives sublime,
And, departing, leave behind us
　　Footprints on the sand of time;

Footprints, that perhaps another,
　　Sailing o'er life's solemn main,
A forlorn and shipwrecked brother,
　　Seeing, shall take heart again.

Let us, then, be up and doing,
　　With a heart for any fate;
Still achieving, still pursuing,
　　Learn to labor and to wait.

## THE STARS

Henry Wadsworth Longfellow

Silently one by one, in the infinite meadows
　　of heaven,
Blossomed the lovely stars, the forget-me-nots
　　of the angels.

—From "Evangeline"

## COUNTERS

Elizabeth Coatsworth

To think I once saw grocery shops
With but a casual eye
And fingered figs and apricots
As one who came to buy!

To think I never dreamed of how
Bananas swayed in rain,
And often looked at oranges
Yet never thought of Spain!

And in those wasted days I saw
No sails above the tea—
For grocery shops were grocery shops,
Not hemispheres to me.

# SUNSET ON THE BEARCAMP

### John Greenleaf Whittier

Touched by a light that hath no name,
   A glory never sung,
Aloft on sky and mountain wall
   Are God's great pictures hung.
How changed the summits vast and old!
   No longer granite-browed,
They melt in rosy mist; the rock
   Is softer than the cloud;
The valley holds its breath; no leaf
   Of all its elms is twirled:
The silence of eternity
   Seems falling on the world.

The pause before the breaking seals
   Of mystery is this;
Yon miracle-play of night and day
   Makes dumb its witnesses.
What unseen altar crowns the hills
   That reach up stair on stair?
What eyes look through, what white wings fan
   These purple veils of air?
What Presence from the heavenly heights
   To those of earth stoops down?
Not vainly Hellas dreamed of gods
   On Ida's snowy crown!

Slow fades the vision of the sky,
   The golden water pales,
And over all the valley-land
   A gray-winged vapor sails . . .
But beauty seen is never lost,
   God's colors all are fast;

The glory of this sunset heaven
  Into my soul has passed,
A sense of gladness unconfined
  To mortal date or clime;
As the soul liveth, it shall live
  Beyond the years of time.

—Selected from "Sunset on the Bearcamp"

## IT COULDN'T BE DONE

### Edgar A. Guest

Somebody said that it couldn't be done,
  But he with a chuckle replied
That "maybe it couldn't," but he would be one
  Who wouldn't say so till he'd tried.
So he buckled right in with the trace of a grin
  On his face. If he worried he hid it.
He started to sing as he tackled the thing
  That couldn't be done, and he did it.

—Selected from "It Couldn't Be Done"

## SHIPS THAT PASS IN THE NIGHT

Henry Wadsworth Longfellow

Ships that pass in the night, and speak each other
    in passing,
Only a signal shown and a distant voice
    in the darkness;
So on the ocean of life we pass and speak
    one another,
Only a look and a voice, then darkness again
    and a silence.

—From "Elizabeth"


## THANATOPSIS

William Cullen Bryant

To him who in the love of Nature holds
Communion with her visible forms, she speaks
A various language; for his gayer hours
She has a voice of gladness, and a smile
And eloquence of beauty, and she glides
Into his darker musings with a mild
And healing sympathy, that steals away
Their sharpness, ere he is aware.

—Selected from "Thanatopsis"

# TREES

### Joyce Kilmer

I think that I shall never see
A poem lovely as a tree.

A tree whose hungry mouth is prest
Against the earth's sweet flowing breast;

A tree that looks at God all day,
And lifts her leafy arms to pray;

A tree that may in Summer wear
A nest of robins in her hair;

Upon whose bosom snow has lain;
Who intimately lives with rain.

Poems are made by fools like me,
But only God can make a tree.

# PEDIGREE

### Emily Dickinson

The pedigree of honey
Does not concern the bee;
A clover, any time, to him
Is aristocracy.

## WHEN THE FROST IS ON THE PUNKIN

James Whitcomb Riley

When the frost is on the punkin and the fodder's in the shock,
And you hear the kyouck and gobble of the struttin' turkey-cock,
And the clackin' of the guineys, and the cluckin' of the hens,
And the rooster's hallylooyer as he tiptoes on the fence;
Oh, it's then's the times a feller is a-feelin' at his best,
With the risin' sun to greet him from a night of peaceful rest,
As he leaves the house, bareheaded, and goes out to feed the stock,
When the frost is on the punkin and the fodder's in the shock.

They's something kind o' harty-like about the atmusfere
When the heat of summer's over and the coolin' fall is here—
Of course we miss the flowers, and the blossums on the trees,
And the mumble of the hummin'-birds and buzzin' of the bees;
But the air's so appetizin'; and the landscape through the haze
Of a crisp and sunny morning of the early autumn days
Is a pictur' that no painter has the colorin' to mock—
When the frost is on the punkin and the fodder's in the shock.

The husky, rusty russel of the tossels of the corn,
And the raspin' of the tangled leaves, as golden as the morn;
The stubble in the furries—kind o' lonesome-like, but still

A-preachin' sermuns to us of the barns they growed to fill;
The straw stack in the medder, and the reaper in the shed;
The hosses in their stalls below—-the clover overhead,—
Oh, it sets my hart a-clickin' like the tickin' of a clock,
When the frost is on the punkin and the fodder's in the shock.

Then your apples all is getherd, and the ones a feller keeps
Is poured around the celler-floor in red and yaller heaps;
And your cider-makin' 's over, and your wimmern-folks is through
With their mince and apple-butter, and their souse and sausage,
        too! . . .
I don't know how to tell it—but ef sich a thing could be
As the Angels wantin' boardin', and they'd call around on *me*—
I'd want to 'commodate 'em—all the whole-indurin' flock—
When the frost is on the punkin and the fodder's in the shock!

## WHENE'ER A NOBLE DEED IS WROUGHT
### Henry Wadsworth Longfellow

Whene'er a noble deed is wrought,
Whene'er is spoken a noble thought,
    Our hearts, in glad surprise,
    To higher levels rise.

Honor to those whose words or deeds
Thus help us in our daily needs,
    And by their overflow
    Raise us from what is low!

—From "Santa Filomena"

# THE SNOW STORM

### Ralph Waldo Emerson

Announced by all the trumpets of the sky,
Arrives the snow, and, driving o'er the fields,
Seems nowhere to alight: the whited air
Hides hills and woods, the river, and the heaven,
And veils the farmhouse at the garden's end.
The sled and traveler stopped, the courier's feet
Delayed, all friends shut out, the housemates sit
Around the radiant fireplace, enclosed
In a tumultuous privacy of storm.

Come see the north wind's masonry.
Out of an unseen quarry evermore
Furnished with tile, the fierce artificer
Curves his white bastions with projected roof
Round every windward stake, or tree, or door.
Speeding, the myriad-handed, his wild work
So fanciful, so savage, nought cares he
For number or proportion. Mockingly,
On coop or kennel he hangs Parian wreaths;
A swan-like form invests the hidden thorn;
Fills up the farmer's lane from wall to wall,
Maugre the farmer's sighs; and at the gate
A tapering turret overtops the work.
And when his hours are numbered, and the world
Is all his own, retiring, as he were not,
Leaves, when the sun appears, astonished Art
To mimic in slow structures, stone by stone,
Built in an age, the mad wind's night-work,
The frolic architecture of the snow.

## WHAT IS GOOD?

John Boyle O'Reilly

"What is the real good?"
I asked in musing mood.

Order, said the law court;
Knowledge, said the school;
Truth, said the wise man;
Pleasure, said the fool;
Love, said the maiden;
Beauty, said the page;
Freedom, said the dreamer;
Home, said the sage;
Fame, said the soldier;
Equity, said the seer;—

Spake my heart full sadly,
"The answer is not here."

Then within my bosom
Softly this I heard:
"Each heart holds the secret;
Kindness is the word."

## THERE IS ALWAYS A BEST WAY

Ralph Waldo Emerson

There is always a best way of doing everything, if it be to boil an egg. Manners are the happy ways of doing things.

—From "Behavior"

# SUCCESS

### Henry Wadsworth Longfellow

We have not wings, we cannot soar;
   But we have feet to scale and climb
By slow degrees, by more and more,
   The cloudy summits of our time.

The mighty pyramids of stone
   That wedge-like cleave the desert airs,
When nearer seen, and better known,
   Are but gigantic flights of stairs.

The distant mountains, that uprear
   Their solid bastions to the skies,
Are crossed by pathways, that appear
   As we to higher levels rise.

The heights by great men reached and kept
   Were not attained by sudden flight,
But they, while their companions slept,
   Were toiling upward in the night.

—From "The Ladder of Saint Augustine"

## WHAT DO WE PLANT?

Henry Abbey

What do we plant when we plant the tree?
We plant the ship, which will cross the sea.
We plant the mast to carry the sails;
We plant the planks to withstand the gales—
The keel, the keelson, the beam, the knee;
We plant the ship when we plant the tree.

What do we plant when we plant the tree?
We plant the houses for you and me.
We plant the rafters, the shingles, the floors,
We plant the studding, the lath, the doors,
The beams and siding, all parts that be;
We plant the house when we plant the tree.

What do we plant when we plant the tree?
A thousand things that we daily see;
We plant the spire that out-towers the crag,
We plant the staff for our country's flag,
We plant the shade, from the hot sun free;
We plant all these when we plant the tree.

# ROADS

Rachel Field

A road might lead to anywhere—
   To harbor towns and quays,
Or to a witch's pointed house
   Hidden by bristly trees.
It might lead past the tailor's door,
   Where he sews with needle and thread,
Or by Miss Pim's, the milliner's,
   With her hats for every head.

It might be a road to a great dark cave,
   With treasure and gold piled high,
Or a road with a mountain tied to its end,
   Blue-humped against the sky.
Oh, a road might lead to anywhere,
   To Mexico or Maine.
But then it might just fool you, and—
   Lead you back home again!

# THE MILLS OF GOD

Henry Wadsworth Longfellow

Though the mills of God grind slowly,
Yet they grind exceeding small;
Though with patience He stands waiting,
With exactness grinds He all.

          —From "Poetic Aphorisms"

# THERE IS NO FRIGATE
## LIKE A BOOK

Emily Dickinson

There is no frigate like a book
To take us lands away,
Nor any coursers like a page
Of prancing poetry.

This traverse may the poorest take
Without oppress of toil;
How frugal is the chariot
That bears a human soul!

# WORTH WHILE

Ella Wheeler Wilcox

It is easy enough to be pleasant,
When life flows by like a song,
But the man worth while is one who will smile,
When everything goes dead wrong.
For the test of the heart is trouble,
And it always comes with the years,
And the smile that is worth the praises of earth
Is the one that shines through tears.

—Selected from "Worth While"

# WOODMAN, SPARE THAT TREE

George Pope Morris

Woodman, spare that tree!
　Touch not a single bough!
In youth it shelter'd me,
　And I'll protect it now.
'Twas my forefather's hand
　That placed it near his cot;
There, woodman, let it stand,
　Thy ax shall harm it not!

That old familiar tree,
　Whose glory and renown
Are spread o'er land and sea,
　And wouldst thou hew it down?
Woodman, forbear thy stroke!
　Cut not its earth-bound ties;
Oh, spare that aged oak,
　Now towering to the skies!

When but an idle boy,
    I sought its grateful shade;
In all their gushing joy
    Here, too, my sisters played.
My mother kissed me here;
    My father pressed my hand—
Forgive this foolish tear,
    But let that old oak stand.

My heart-strings round thee cling,
    Close as thy bark, old friend!
Here shall the wild-bird sing,
    And still thy branches bend.
Old tree! the storm still brave!
    And, woodman, leave the spot;
While I've a hand to save,
    Thy ax shall harm it not.

## THE OLD FRIEND

Oliver Wendell Holmes

There is no friend like the old friend, who
    has shared our morning days,
No greeting like his welcome, no homage
    like his praise.

—From "No Time Like the Old Time"

## WHITTLING

### John Pierpont

The Yankee boy, before he's sent to school,
Well knows the mysteries of that magic tool,
The pocketknife.  To that this wistful eye
Turns, while he hears his mother's lullaby;
His hoarded cents he gladly gives to get it,
Then leaves no stone unturned till he can whet it;
And in the education of the lad
No little part that implement hath had.
His pocketknife to the young whittler brings
A growing knowledge of material things.

—Selected from "Whittling"

## SALUTE TO OUR FLAG

I pledge allegiance to the flag of the United States of America, and to the Republic for which it stands, one nation under God, indivisible, with liberty and justice for all.

# THE SCOUT OATH

On my honor I will do my best—
    To do my duty to God and my country, and to obey
      the Scout law;
    To help other people at all times;
    To keep myself physically strong, mentally awake,
      and morally straight.

# THE GIRL SCOUT PROMISE

On my honor, I will try:
    To serve God,
    My country and mankind,
    And to live by the Girl Scout Law.

# 3

# AMERICA

mister mckee

## COLUMBUS

Joaquin Miller

Behind him lay the gray Azores,
Behind the Gates of Hercules;
Before him not the ghost of shores,
Before him only shoreless seas.
The good mate said: "Now must we pray,
For lo! the very stars are gone.
Brave Adm'r'l, speak; what shall I say?"
"Why, say, 'Sail on! sail on! and on!'"

"My men grow mutinous day by day;
My men grow ghastly wan and weak."
The stout mate thought of home; a spray
Of salt wave washed his swarthy cheek.
"What shall I say, brave Adm'r'l, say,
If we sight naught but seas at dawn?"
"Why, you shall say at break of day:
'Sail on! sail on! sail on! and on!'"

They sailed and sailed, as winds might blow,
Until at last the blanched mate said:

"Why, now not even God would know
Should I and all my men fall dead.
These very winds forget their way,
For God from these dread seas is gone.
Now speak, brave Adm'r'l, speak and say—"
He said, "Sail on! sail on! and on!"

They sailed. They sailed. Then spake the mate:
"This mad sea shows his teeth tonight.
He curls his lip, he lies in wait,
With lifted teeth, as if to bite!
Brave Adm'r'l, say but one good word:
What shall we do when hope is gone?"
The words leapt like a leaping sword:
"Sail on! sail on! sail on! and on!"

Then pale and worn, he kept his deck,
And peered through darkness. Ah, that night
Of all dark nights! And then a speck—
A light! A light! A light! A light!
It grew, a starlit flag unfurled!
It grew to be Time's burst of dawn.
He gained a world; he gave that world
Its grandest lesson: "On! sail on!"

## HIAWATHA'S CHILDHOOD

Henry Wadsworth Longfellow

By the shores of Gitchee Gumee,
By the shining Big-Sea-Water,
Stood the wigwam of Nokomis,
Daughter of the Moon, Nokomis.
Dark behind it rose the forest,
Rose the black and gloomy pine-trees,
Rose the firs with cones upon them;
Bright before it beat the water,
Beat the clear and sunny water,
Beat the shining Big-Sea-Water.
　　There the wrinkled old Nokomis
Nursed the little Hiawatha,
Rocked him in his linden cradle,
Bedded soft in moss and rushes,
Safely bound with reindeer sinews;
Stilled his fretful wail by saying,
"Hush! the Naked Bear will hear thee!"
Lulled him into slumber, singing,
"Ewa-yea! my little owlet!
Who is this, that lights the wigwam?
With his great eyes lights the wigwam?

Ewa-yea! my little owlet!"
   Many things Nokomis taught him
Of the stars that shine in heaven;
Showed him Ishkoodah, the comet,
Ishkoodah, with fiery tresses;
Showed the Death-Dance of the spirits,
Warriors with their plumes and war-clubs,
Flaring far away to northward
In the frosty nights of Winter;
Showed the broad white road in heaven,
Pathway of the ghosts, the shadows,
Running straight across the heavens,
Crowded with the ghosts, the shadows.

   At the door on summer evenings
Sat the little Hiawatha;
Heard the whispering of the pine-trees,
Heard the lapping of the waters,
Sounds of music, words of wonder;
"Minne-wawa!" said the pine-trees,
"Mudway-aushka!" said the water.
   Saw the firefly, Wah-wah-taysee,
Flitting through the dusk of evening,
With the twinkle of its candle
Lighting up the brakes and bushes,
And he sang the song of children,
Sang the song Nokomis taught him:

"Wah-wah-taysee, little firefly,
Little, flitting, white-fire insect,
Little, dancing, white-fire creature,
Light me with your little candle,
Ere upon my bed I lay me,
Ere in sleep I close my eyelids!"
   Saw the moon rise from the water
Rippling, rounding from the water,
Saw the flecks and shadows on it,
Whispered, "What is that, Nokomis?"
And the good Nokomis answered:
"Once a warrior, very angry,
Seized his grandmother, and threw her
Up into the sky at midnight;
Right against the moon he threw her;
'Tis her body that you see there."

   Then the little Hiawatha
Learned of every bird its language,
Learned their names and all their secrets,
How they built their nests in Summer,
Where they hid themselves in Winter,
Talked with them whene'er he met them,
Called them "Hiawatha's Chickens."
   Of all beasts he learned the language,
Learned their names and all their secrets,
How the beavers built their lodges,
Where the squirrels hid their acorns,

How the reindeer ran so swiftly,
Why the rabbit was so timid,
Talked with them whene'er he met them,
Called them "Hiawatha's Brothers."

—From "The Song of Hiawatha"

## HIAWATHA'S SAILING

Henry Wadsworth Longfellow

"Give me of your bark, O Birch-tree!
Of your yellow bark, O Birch-tree!
Growing by the rushing river,
Tall and stately in the valley!
I a light canoe will build me,
Build a swift Cheemaun for sailing,
That shall float upon the river,
Like a yellow leaf in Autumn,
Like a yellow water-lily!
  "Lay aside your cloak, O Birch-tree!
Lay aside your white-skin wrapper,
For the Summer-time is coming,
And the sun is warm in heaven,
And you need no white-skin wrapper!"
  Thus aloud cried Hiawatha
In the solitary forest,
By the rushing Taquamenaw,

When the birds were singing gayly,
In the Moon of Leaves were singing,
And the sun, from sleep awaking,
Started up and said, "Behold me!
Geezis, the great Sun, behold me!"
    And the tree with all its branches
Rustled in the breeze of morning,
Saying, with a sigh of patience,
"Take my cloak, O Hiawatha!"
    With his knife the tree he girdled;
Just beneath its lowest branches,
Just above the roots, he cut it,
Till the sap came oozing outward;
Down the trunk, from top to bottom,
Sheer he cleft the bark asunder,
With a wooden wedge he raised it,
Stripped it from the trunk unbroken.
    "Give me of your boughs, O Cedar!
Of your strong and pliant branches,
My canoe to make more steady,
Make more strong and firm beneath me!"
    Through the summit of the Cedar
Went a sound, a cry of horror,
Went a murmur of resistance;
But it whispered, bending downward,
"Take my boughs, O Hiawatha!"
    Down he hewed the boughs of cedar,
Shaped them straightway to framework,
Like two bows he formed and shaped them,
Like two bended bows together.
    "Give me of your roots, O Tamarack!
Of your fibrous roots, O Larch-tree!
My canoe to bind together,
So to bind the ends together
That the water may not enter,

That the river may not wet me!"
    And the Larch, with all its fibers,
Shivered in the air of morning,
Touched his forehead with its tassels,
Said, with one long sigh of sorrow,
"Take them all, O Hiawatha!"

    From the earth he tore the fibers,
Tore the tough roots of the Larch-tree,
Closely sewed the bark together,
Bound it closely to the framework.
    "Give me of your balm, O Fir-tree!
Of your balsam and your resin,
So to close the seams together
That the water may not enter,
That the river may not wet me!"
    And the Fir-tree, tall and somber,
Sobbed through all its robes of darkness,
Rattled like a shore with pebbles,
Answered wailing, answered weeping,
"Take my balm, O Hiawatha!"
    And he took the tears of balsam,
Took the resin of the Fir-tree,
Smeared therewith each seam and fissure,

Made each crevice safe from water.
　"Give me of your quills, O Hedgehog!
All your quills, O Kagh, the Hedgehog!
I will make a necklace of them,
Make a girdle for my beauty,
And two stars to deck her bosom!"
　From a hollow tree the Hedgehog
With his sleepy eyes looked at him,
Shot his shining quills, like arrows,
Saying with a drowsy murmur,
Through the tangle of his whiskers,
"Take my quills, O Hiawatha!"
　From the ground the quills he gathered,
All the little shining arrows,
Stained them red and blue and yellow,
With the juice of roots and berries;
Into his canoe he wrought them,
Round its waist a shining girdle,
Round its bows a gleaming necklace,
On its breast two stars resplendent.
　Thus the Birch Canoe was builded
In the valley, by the river,
In the bosom of the forest;
And the forest's life was in it,
All its mystery and its magic,
All the lightness of the birch-tree,
All the toughness of the cedar,
All the larch's supple sinews;
And it floated on the river
Like a yellow leaf in Autumn,
Like a yellow water-lily.
　Paddles none he had or needed,
For his thoughts as paddles served him,
And his wishes served to guide him;
Swift or slow at will he glided,

Veered to right or left at pleasure.
Then he called aloud to Kwasind,
To his friend, the strong man, Kwasind,
Saying, "Help me clear this river
Of its sunken logs and sand-bars."
Straight into the river Kwasind
Plunged as if he were an otter,
Dived as if he were a beaver,
Stood up to his waist in water,
To his arm-pits in the river,
Swam and shouted in the river,
Tugged at sunken logs and branches,
With his hands he scooped the sand-bars,
With his feet the ooze and tangle.
And thus sailed my Hiawatha
Down the rushing Taquamenaw,
Sailed through all its bends and windings,
Sailed through all its deeps and shallows,
While his friend, the strong man, Kwasind,
Swam the deeps, the shallows waded.
Up and down the river went they,
In and out among its islands,
Cleared its bed of root and sand-bar,
Dragged the dead trees from its channel,
Made its passage safe and certain,
Made a pathway for the people,
From its springs among the mountains,
To the waters of Pauwating,
To the bay of Taquamenaw.

—From "The Song of Hiawatha"

# THE LANDING OF THE PILGRIM FATHERS

*(November 19, 1620)*

Felicia Dorothea Hemans

The breaking waves dashed high
On a stern and rock-bound coast,
And the woods, against a stormy sky,
Their giant branches tossed;

And the heavy night hung dark
The hills and waters o'er,
When a band of exiles moored their bark
On a wild New England shore.

Not as the conqueror comes,
They, the true-hearted, came;
Not with the roll of the stirring drums,
And the trumpet that sings of fame;

Not as the flying come,
In silence and in fear;—
They shook the depths of the desert's gloom
With their hymns of lofty cheer.

Amidst the storm they sang,
And the stars heard, and the sea;
And the sounding aisles of the dim woods rang
To the anthem of the free!

The ocean-eagle soared
From his nest by the white wave's foam,
And the rocking pines of the forest roared;
This was their welcome home!

There were men with hoary hair
Amidst that pilgrim band;
Why had they come to wither there,
Away from their childhood's land?

There was woman's fearless eye,
Lit by her deep love's truth;
There was manhood's brow, serenely high,
And the fiery heart of youth.

What sought they thus afar?
Bright jewels of the mine?
The wealth of seas, the spoils of war?—
They sought a faith's pure shrine!

Aye, call it holy ground,
The soil where first they trod!
They left unstained what there they found—
Freedom to worship God!

## THE INSCRIPTION ON
## PLYMOUTH ROCK MONUMENT

THIS MONUMENT MARKS THE FIRST
BURYING GROUND IN PLYMOUTH OF
THE PASSENGERS OF THE MAYFLOWER

Here, under cover of darkness, the fast dwindling company laid their dead, leveling the earth above them lest the Indians should know how many were the graves. Reader! History records no nobler venture for faith and freedom than of this Pilgrim band. In weariness and painfulness, in watchings, often in hunger and cold, they laid the foundations of a state wherein every man, through countless ages, should have liberty to worship God in his own way. May their example inspire thee to do thy part in perpetuating and spreading the lofty ideals of our republic throughout the world!

## A RULE

Labor to keep alive in your breast that little spark of celestial fire —conscience.

—From the Copy-book of George Washington

## GEORGE WASHINGTON
## AND THE CHERRY TREE

Mason Locke ("Parson") Weems

The following anecdote is a case in point. It is too valuable to be lost, and too true to be doubted; for it was communicated to me by the same excellent lady to whom I am indebted for the last.

"When George," said she, "was about six years old, he was made the wealthy master of a hatchet! of which, like most little boys, he was immoderately fond, and was constantly going about chopping every thing that came in his way. One day, in the garden, where he often amused himself hacking his mother's pea-sticks, he unluckily tried the edge of his hatchet on the body of a beautiful young English cherry-tree, which he barked so terribly, that I don't believe the tree ever got the better of it. The next morning the old gentleman, finding out what had befallen his tree, which, by the by, was a great favorite, came into the house; and with much warmth asked for the mischievous author, declaring at the same time, that he would not have taken five guineas for his tree. Nobody could tell him anything about it. Presently George and his hatchet made their appearance. 'George,' said his father, 'do you know who killed that beautiful little cherry-tree yonder in the garden?' This was a tough question; and George staggered under it for a moment; but quickly recovered himself; and looking at his father, with the sweet face of youth brightened with the inexpressible charm of all-conquering truth, he bravely cried out, 'I can't tell a lie, Pa. You know I can't tell a lie. I did cut it with my hatchet.'—'Run to my arms, you dearest boy,' cried his father in transports, 'run to my arms; glad am I, George, that you killed my tree; for you have paid me for it a thousand fold. Such an act of heroism in my son is more worth than a thousand trees, though blossomed with silver, and their fruits of purest gold.'"

—From *The Life of George Washington*

## HERE IS MY CREED

### Benjamin Franklin

Here is my creed.
>    I believe in one God, the creator of the Universe.
>    That He governs it by His Providence.
>    That He ought to be worshipped.
>    That the most acceptable service we render to Him
>        is doing good to His other children.
>    That the soul of man is immortal, and will be treated
>        with justice in another life respecting its conduct
>        in this.

# SAYINGS OF "POOR RICHARD"
### Benjamin Franklin

Keep conscience clear, then never fear.

\* \* \*

Keep thy shop, and thy shop will keep thee.

\* \* \*

He that would live in peace and at ease, must not speak all he knows, nor judge all he sees.

\* \* \*

The use of money is all the advantage there is in having money.

\* \* \*

Hide not your talents, they for use were made. What's a sun-dial in the shade?

\* \* \*

Great beauty, great strength, and great riches are really and truly of no great use; a right heart exceeds all.

\* \* \*

We are not so sensible of the greatest health as of the least sickness.

\* \* \*

A slip of the foot you may soon recover, but a slip of the tongue you may never get over.

\* \* \*

Early to bed and early to rise, makes a man healthy, wealthy, and wise.

\* \* \*

Don't throw stones at your neighbors', if your own windows are glass.

\* \* \*

God helps them that help themselves.

\* \* \*

He that scatters thorns, let him not go barefoot.

\* \* \*

Reading makes a full man—meditation a profound man—discourse a clear man.

\* \* \*

For want of a nail the shoe is lost; for want of a shoe the horse is lost; for want of a horse the rider is lost.

\* \* \*

Dost thou love life? Then do not squander time; for that's the stuff life is made of.

—From *Poor Richard's Almanack*

[ 169 ]

## YANKEE DOODLE

Anonymous

Father and I went down to camp,
Along with Cap'n Goodwin,
And there we saw the men and boys,
As thick as hasty puddin'!

*Chorus:*
Yankee Doodle, keep it up,
Yankee Doodle dandy,
Mind the music and the step,
And with the girls be handy!

And there we see a thousand men,
As rich as Squire David;
And what they wasted ev'ry day,
I wish it could be saved.

And there I see a swamping gun,
Large as a log of maple,
Upon a deuced little cart,
A load for father's cattle.

And every time they shoot it off,
It takes a horn of powder,
And makes a noise like father's gun,
Only a nation louder.

I went as nigh to one myself,
As 'Siah's underpinning;
And father went as nigh ag'in,
I thought the deuce was in him.

We saw a little barrel, too,
The heads were made of leather;
They knocked upon it with little clubs,
And called the folks together.

And there they'd fife away like fun,
And play on cornstalk fiddles,
And some had ribbons red as blood,
All bound around their middles.

The troopers, too, would gallop up
And fire right in our faces;
It scared me almost to death
To see them run such races.

—Selected from "Yankee Doodle"

## BE COURTEOUS TO ALL

George Washington

Be courteous to all, but intimate with few, and let those few be well tried before you give them your confidence. True friendship is a plant of slow growth, and must undergo and withstand the shocks of adversity before it is entitled to the appellation.

[ 171 ]

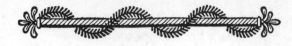

## GIVE ME LIBERTY, OR GIVE ME DEATH!
### Patrick Henry

. . . . There is a just God who presides over the destinies of nations; and who will raise up friends to fight our battles for us. The battle, sir, is not to the strong alone; it is to the vigilant, the active, the brave. Besides, sir, we have no election. If we were base enough to desire it, it is now too late to retire from the contest. There is no retreat, but in submission and slavery! Our chains are forged! Their clanking may be heard on the plains of Boston! The war is inevitable—and let it come! I repeat it, sir, let it come!

It is in vain, sir, to extenuate the matter. Gentlemen may cry, Peace, Peace—but there is no peace. The war is actually begun! The next gale that sweeps from the north will bring to our ears the clash of resounding arms! Our brethren are already in the field! Why stand we here idle? What is it that gentlemen wish? What would they have? Is life so dear, or peace so sweet, as to be purchased at the price of chains and slavery? Forbid it, Almighty God! I know not what course others may take; but as for me, give me liberty, or give me death!

—From *The Call to Arms* (A speech delivered March 23, 1775, to the Virginia House of Burgesses, Richmond, Virginia)

# THESE ARE THE TIMES
# THAT TRY MEN'S SOULS
## Thomas Paine

These are the times that try men's souls. The summer soldier and the sunshine patriot will, in this crisis, shrink from the service of their country; but he that stands it *now*, deserves the love and thanks of man and woman. Tyranny, like hell, is not easily conquered; yet we have this consolation with us, that the harder the conflict, the more glorious the triumph. What we obtain too cheap, we esteem too lightly; it is dearness only that gives everything its value. Heaven knows how to put a proper price upon its goods; and it would be strange, indeed, if so celestial an article as FREEDOM should not be highly rated.

—From "The American Crisis"

## PAUL REVERE'S RIDE

Henry Wadsworth Longfellow

Listen, my children, and you shall hear
Of the midnight ride of Paul Revere,
On the eighteenth of April, in Seventy-five;
Hardly a man is now alive
Who remembers that famous day and year.

He said to his friend, "If the British march
By land or sea from the town tonight,
Hang a lantern aloft in the belfry arch
Of the North Church tower as a signal light—
One, if by land, and two, if by sea;
And I on the opposite shore will be,
Ready to ride and spread the alarm
Through every Middlesex village and farm,
For the country folk to be up and to arm."

Then he said, "Good night!" and with muffled oar
Silently rowed to the Charlestown shore,
Just as the moon rose over the bay,
Where swinging wide at her moorings lay

The *Somerset*, British man-of-war;
A phantom ship, with each mast and spar
Across the moon like a prison bar,
And a huge black hulk, that was magnified
By its own reflection in the tide.

Meanwhile, his friend, through alley and street,
Wanders and watches, with eager ears,
Till in the silence around him he hears
The muster of men at the barrack door,
And the measured tread of the grenadiers,
Marching down to their boats on the shore.

Then he climbed to the tower of the Old North Church,
By the wooden stairs, with stealthy tread,
To the belfry-chamber overhead,
And startled the pigeons from their perch
On the somber rafters, that round him made
Masses and moving shapes of shade—
By the trembling ladder, steep and tall,
To the highest window in the wall,
Where he paused to listen and look down
A moment on the roofs of the town,
And the moonlight flowing over all.

Beneath in the churchyard, lay the dead,
In their night-encampment on the hill,
Wrapped in silence so deep and still
That he could hear, like a sentinel's tread,
The watchful night-wind, as it went
Creeping along from tent to tent,
And seeming to whisper, "All is well!"
A moment only he feels the spell
Of the place and the hour, and the secret dread
Of the lonely belfry and the dead;

For suddenly all his thoughts are bent
On a shadowy something far away,
Where the river widens to meet the bay—
A line of black that bends and floats
On the rising tide, like a bridge of boats.

Meanwhile, impatient to mount and ride,
Booted and spurred, with a heavy stride
On the opposite shore walked Paul Revere.
Now he patted his horse's side,
Now gazed at the landscape far and near,
Then, impetuous, stamped the earth,
And turned and tightened his saddle girth;
But mostly he watched with eager search
The belfry tower of the Old North Church,
As it rose above the graves on the hill,
Lonely and spectral and somber and still.
And lo! as he looks, on the belfry's height
A glimmer, and then a gleam of light!
He springs to the saddle, the bridle he turns,
But lingers and gazes, till full on his sight
A second lamp in the belfry burns!

A hurry of hoofs in a village street,
A shape in the moonlight, a bulk in the dark,
And beneath, from the pebbles, in passing, a spark
Struck out by a steed flying fearless and fleet:
That was all! And yet, through the gloom and the light,
The fate of a nation was riding that night;
And the spark struck out by that steed, in his flight,
Kindled the land into flame with its heat.

He has left the village and mounted the steep,
And beneath him, tranquil and broad and deep,
Is the Mystic, meeting the ocean tides;

And under the alders that skirt its edge,
Now soft on the sand, now loud on the ledge,
Is heard the tramp of his steed as he rides.

It was twelve by the village clock,
When he crossed the bridge into Medford town.
He heard the crowing of the cock,
And the barking of the farmer's dog,
And felt the damp of the river fog,
That rises after the sun goes down.
It was one by the village clock,
When he galloped into Lexington.
He saw the gilded weathercock
Swim in the moonlight as he passed,
And the meeting-house windows, blank and bare,
Gaze at him with a spectral glare,
As if they already stood aghast
At the bloody work they would look upon.

It was two by the village clock,
When he came to the bridge in Concord town.
He heard the bleating of the flock,
And the twitter of birds among the trees,
And felt the breath of the morning breeze
Blowing over the meadows brown.
And one was safe and asleep in his bed
Who at the bridge would be first to fall,
Who that day would be lying dead,
Pierced by a British musket-ball.

You know the rest. In the books you have read
How the British Regulars fired and fled—
How the farmers gave them ball for ball,
From behind each fence and farmyard wall,
Chasing the red-coats down the lane,

Then crossing the fields to emerge again
Under the trees at the turn of the road,
And only pausing to fire and load.

So through the night rode Paul Revere;
And so through the night went his cry of alarm
To every Middlesex village and farm—
A cry of defiance and not of fear,
A voice in the darkness, a knock at the door,
And a word that shall echo for evermore!
For, borne on the night-wind of the Past,
Through all our history, to the last,
In the hour of darkness and peril and need,
The people will awaken and listen to hear
The hurrying hoof-beats of that steed,
And the midnight message of Paul Revere.

# THE CONCORD HYMN

### Ralph Waldo Emerson

By the rude bridge that arched the flood,
Their flag to April's breeze unfurled,
Here once the embattled farmers stood,
And fired the shot heard round the world.

The foe long since in silence slept;
Alike the conqueror silent sleeps;
And Time the ruined bridge has swept
Down the dark stream which seaward creeps.

On this green bank, by this soft stream,
We set today a votive stone;
That memory may their dead redeem,
When, like our sires, our sons are gone.

Spirit, that made those spirits dare
To die, and leave their children free,
Bid Time and Nature gently spare
The shaft we raise to them and thee.

## WARREN'S ADDRESS

### John Pierpont

Stand! the ground's your own, my braves!
Will ye give it up to slaves?
Will ye look for greener graves?
    Hope ye mercy still?
What's the mercy despots feel?
Hear it in that battle-peal!
Read it on yon bristling steel!
    Ask it—ye who will.

Fear ye foes who kill for hire?
Will ye to your *homes* retire?
Look behind you!—they're afire!
    And, before you, see
Who have done it! From the vale
On they come!—and will ye quail?
Leaden rain and iron hail
    Let their welcome be!

In the God of battle trust!
Die we may—and die we must:
But, oh where can dust to dust
    Be consigned so well,
As where Heaven its dews shall shed
On the martyr'd patriot's bed,
And the rocks shall raise their head
    Of his deeds to tell?

(Major General Joseph Warren was killed at the Battle of Bunker Hill)

[ 180 ]

# THE DECLARATION OF INDEPENDENCE

When, in the course of human events, it becomes necessary for one people to dissolve the political bands which have connected them with another, and to assume among the powers of the earth, the separate and equal station to which the laws of nature and of nature's God entitle them, a decent respect to the opinions of mankind requires that they should declare the causes which impel them to the separation.

We hold these truths to be self-evident: That all men are created equal, that they are endowed by their Creator with certain unalienable rights, that among these are life, liberty, and the pursuit of happiness; that, to secure these rights, Governments are instituted among men, deriving their just powers from the consent of the governed; that, whenever any form of Government becomes destructive of these ends, it is the right of the people to alter or to abolish it, and to institute new Government, laying its foundation on such principles, and organizing its powers in such form, as to them shall seem most likely to effect their safety and happiness.

—From *The Declaration of Independence* (July 4, 1776)

## ON FREEDOM OF THOUGHT
Samuel Adams

Freedom of thought and the right of private judgment in matters of conscience, driven from every other corner of the earth, direct their course to this happy country as their last asylum.

## TO THE AMERICAN TROOPS
## BEFORE THE BATTLE OF LONG ISLAND
George Washington

The time is now near at hand which must probably determine whether Americans are to be freemen or slaves; whether they are to have any property they can call their own; whether their houses and farms are to be pillaged and destroyed, and themselves consigned to a state of wretchedness from which no human efforts will deliver them. The fate of unborn millions will now depend, under God, on the courage and conduct of this army. Our cruel and unrelenting enemy leaves us only the choice of a brave resistance, or the most abject submission. We have, therefore, to resolve to conquer or to die.

## NATHAN HALE

Francis Miles Finch

To drum-beat and heart-beat,
  A soldier marches by;
There is color in his cheek,
  There is courage in his eye,
Yet to drum-beat and heart-beat
  In a moment he must die.

By starlight and moonlight,
  He seeks the Briton's camp;
He hears the rustling flag,
  And the armed sentry's tramp;
And the starlight and moonlight
  His silent wanderings lamp.

With slow tread and still tread,
  He scans the tented line;
And he counts the battery guns
  By the gaunt and shadowy pine;

[ 183 ]

And his slow tread and still tread
  Gives no warning sign.

The dark wave, the plumed wave,
  It meets his eager glance;
And it sparkles 'neath the stars,
  Like the glimmer of a lance—
A dark wave, a plumed wave,
  On an emerald expanse.

A sharp clang, a steel clang,
  And terror in the sound!
For the sentry, falcon-eyed,
  In the camp a spy hath found;
With a sharp clang, a steel clang,
  The patriot is bound.

With calm brow, and steady brow,
  He listens to his doom;
In his look there is no fear,
  Nor a shadow-trace of gloom;
But with calm brow and steady brow,
  He robes him for the tomb.

In the long night, the still night,
  He kneels upon the sod;
And the brutal guards withhold
  E'en the solemn Word of God!
In the long night, the still night,
  He walks where Christ hath trod.

'Neath the blue morn, the sunny morn,
  He dies upon the tree;
And he mourns that he can lose
  But one life for Liberty;

And in the blue morn, the sunny morn,
    His spirit wings are free.

But his last words, his message-words,
    They burn, lest friendly eye
Should read how proud and calm
    A patriot could die,
With his last words, his dying words,
    A soldier's battle-cry.

From the Fame-leaf and Angel-leaf,
    From monument and urn,
The sad of earth, the glad of heaven,
    His tragic fate shall learn;
But on Fame-leaf and Angel-leaf
    The name of HALE shall burn.


## SONG OF MARION'S MEN

### William Cullen Bryant

Our band is few, but true and tried,
    Our leader frank and bold;
The British soldier trembles
    When Marion's name is told.
Our fortress is the good greenwood,
    Our tent the cypress tree;
We know the forest round us,
    As seamen know the sea.
We know its walls of thorny vines,
    Its glades of reedy grass,
Its safe and silent islands
    Within the dark morass.

—Selected from "The Song of Marion's Men"

## NATHAN HALE SAID

I only regret that I have but one life to lose for my country.
—(His last words; September 22, 1776)

## THE RAPID PROGRESS OF TRUE SCIENCE
Benjamin Franklin

The rapid progress *true* science now makes, occasions my regretting sometimes that I was born so soon. It is impossible to imagine the height to which may be carried, in a thousand years, the power of man over matter. We may perhaps learn to deprive large masses of their gravity, and give them absolute levity, for the sake of easy transport. Agriculture may diminish its labor and double its produce; all diseases may by sure means be prevented or cured, not excepting even that of old age, and our lives lengthened at pleasure beyond even the antediluvian standard. O that *moral* science were in as fair a way of improvement, that men would cease to be wolves to one another, and that human beings would at length learn what they now improperly call humanity.

—From a letter written to Joseph Priestly, the English chemist, in 1780

## LET US RAISE A STANDARD
George Washington

Let us raise a standard to which the wise and honest can repair; the rest is in the hands of God.

—From a speech to the Constitutional Convention, 1787

## PREAMBLE TO THE CONSTITUTION
## OF THE UNITED STATES

We, the People of the United States, in order to form a more perfect union, establish justice, insure domestic tranquillity, provide for the common defense, promote the general welfare, and secure the blessings of liberty to ourselves and our posterity, do ordain and establish this CONSTITUTION for the United States of America.

## THE AMERICAN FLAG
### Joseph Rodman Drake

#### I

When Freedom, from her mountain height,
   Unfurled her standard to the air,
She tore the azure robe of night,
   And set the stars of glory there!
She mingled with its gorgeous dyes
The milky baldric of the skies,
And striped its pure, celestial white
With streakings of the morning light;
Then, from his mansion in the sun,
She called her eagle-bearer down,
And gave into his mighty hand,
   The symbol of her chosen land.

## II

Majestic monarch of the cloud!
   Who rear'st aloft thy regal form,
To hear the tempest-trumpings loud,
And see the lightning-lances driven,
   When strive the warriors of the storm,
And rolls the thunder-drum of heaven—
Child of the sun! to thee 'tis given
   To guard the banner of the free,
To hover in the sulphur smoke,
To ward away the battle stroke,
And bid its blendings shine afar,
Like rainbows on the cloud of war,
   The harbingers of victory!

## III

Flag of the brave! thy folds shall fly,
The sign of hope and triumph high,
When speaks the signal-trumpet tone,
And the long line comes gleaming on,
Ere yet the life-blood, warm and wet,
Has dimmed the glistening bayonet,
Each soldier's eye shall brightly turn
To where thy sky-born glories burn,
And, as his springing steps advance,
Catch war and vengeance from the glance!
And when the cannon-mouthings loud
Heave in wild wreaths the battle-shroud,
And gory sabers rise and fall,
Like shoots of flame on midnight's pall;
Then shall thy meteor-glances glow,
   And cowering foes shall sink beneath
Each gallant arm that strikes below
   That lovely messenger of death.

## IV

Flag of the seas! on ocean wave
Thy stars shall glitter o'er the brave;
When Death, careering on the gale,
Sweeps darkly round the bellied sail,
And frighted waves rush wildly back
Before the broadside's reeling rack,
Each dying wanderer of the sea
Shall look, at once, to heaven and thee,
And smile, to see thy splendors fly
In triumph, o'er his closing eye.

## V

Flag of the free! heart's hope and home,
   By angel hands to valor given!
Thy stars have lit the welkin dome,
   And all thy hues were born in heaven.
(And fixed as yonder orb divine,
   That saw thy bannered blaze unfurled,
Shall thy proud stars resplendent shine,
   The guard and glory of the world.)
Forever float that standard sheet!
   Where breathes the foe but falls before us,
With Freedom's soil beneath our feet,
And Freedom's banner streaming o'er us!

# AMERICA

### Samuel Francis Smith

My country, 'tis of thee,
Sweet land of liberty,
  Of thee I sing;
Land where my fathers died,
Land of the Pilgrims' pride,
From every mountain-side
  Let Freedom ring.

My native country, thee,
Land of the noble free—
  Thy name I love;
I love thy rocks and rills,
Thy woods and templed hills:
My heart with rapture thrills
  Like that above.

Let music swell the breeze,
And ring from all the trees
  Sweet Freedom's song;
Let mortal tongues awake,
Let all that breathe partake,
Let rocks their silence break—
  The sound prolong.

Our fathers' God, to Thee,
Author of liberty,
  To Thee we sing;
Long may our land be bright
With Freedom's holy light;
Protect us by Thy might,
  Great God, our King.

## FIRST IN WAR—FIRST IN PEACE

Henry Lee

First in war, first in peace, and first in the hearts of his country-men, he was second to none in the humble and endearing scenes of private life. Pious, just, humane, temperate and sincere; uniform, dignified and commanding, his example was as edifying to all around him, as were the effects of that example lasting.

—From the funeral oration in honor of George Washington (December 26, 1799)

## THE INSCRIPTION AT MOUNT VERNON

Washington, the brave, the wise, the good,
Supreme in war, in council, and in peace,
Valiant without ambition, discreet without fear,
Confident without presumption.
In disaster, calm; in success, moderate;
    in all, himself.
The hero, the patriot, the Christian.
The father of nations, the friend of mankind,
Who, when he had won all, renounced all,
And sought in the bosom of his family
    and of nature, retirement,
And in the hope of religion, immortality.

# FOURTH OF JULY ODE

James Russell Lowell

**I**

Our fathers fought for Liberty,
They struggled long and well,
History of their deeds can tell—
But did they leave us free?

**II**

Are we free from vanity,
Free from pride, and free from self,
Free from love of power and pelf,
From everything that's beggarly?

**III**

Are we free from stubborn will,
From low hate and malice small,
From opinion's tyrant thrall?
Are none of us our own slaves still?

**IV**

Are we free to speak our thought,
To be happy, and be poor,
Free to enter Heaven's door,
To live and labor as we ought?

### V

Are we then made free at last
From the fear of what men say,
Free to reverence Today,
Free from the slavery of the Past?

### VI

Our fathers fought for liberty,
They struggled long and well,
History of their deeds can tell—
But *ourselves* must set us free.

## THOMAS JEFFERSON SAID

When a man assumes a public trust, he should consider himself as public property.

\* \* \*

I am ready to say to every human being, "Thou art my brother," and to offer him the hand of concord and amity.

# HAIL, COLUMBIA

### Joseph Hopkinson

Hail! Columbia, happy land!
Hail! ye heroes, heaven-born band,
Who fought and bled in freedom's cause,
And when the storm of war was gone,
Enjoyed the peace your valor won;
Let independence be your boast,
Ever mindful what it cost,
Ever grateful for the prize,
Let its altar reach the skies.

*Chorus:*
>    Firm, united let us be,
>    Rallying round our liberty,
>    As a band of brothers joined,
>    Peace and safety we shall find.

Immortal patriots, rise once more!
Defend your rights, defend your shore;
Let no rude foe with impious hand,

Invade the shrine where sacred lies
Of toil and blood the well-earned prize;
While offering peace, sincere and just,
In heaven we place a manly trust,
That truth and justice will prevail,
And every scheme of bondage fail.

Sound, sound the trump of fame!
Let Washington's great name
Ring through the world with loud applause!
Let every clime to freedom dear
Listen with a joyful ear;
With equal skill, with steady power,
He governs in the fearful hour
Of horrid war, or guides with ease
The happier time of honest peace.

Behold the chief, who now commands,
Once more to serve his country stands,
The rock on which the storm will beat!
But armed in virtue, firm and true,
His hopes are fixed on heaven and you.
When hope was sinking in dismay,
When gloom obscured Columbia's day,
His steady mind, from changes free,
Resolved on death or liberty.

## YOUR COUNTRY
### Edward Everett Hale

"Youngster, let that show you what it is to be without a family, without a home, and without a country. . . . Stick by your family, boy; forget you have a self, while you do everything for them. . . . And for your country, boy, and for that flag, never dream a dream but of serving her as she bids you, though the service carry you through a thousand hells. No matter what happens to you, no matter who flatters you or who abuses you, never look at another flag, never let a night pass but you pray God to bless that flag. Remember, boy, that behind all these men you have to do with, behind officers and Government and people even, there is the Country Herself, your Country, and that you belong to Her as you belong to your own mother. Stand by Her, boy, as you would stand by your mother!"

—From *The Man Without a Country*


## WELL, DID YOU HEAR?
### Edmund Vance Cooke

Well, did you hear? Tom Lincoln's wife today,
The devil's luck for folks as poor as they!
Poor Tom! Poor Nance!
Poor youngun born without a chance!

## OLD IRONSIDES

Oliver Wendell Holmes

Ay, tear her tattered ensign down!
　　Long has it waved on high,
And many an eye has danced to see
　　That banner in the sky;
Beneath it rung the battle shout,
　　And burst the cannon's roar;—
The meteor of the ocean air
　　Shall sweep the clouds no more!

Her deck, once red with heroes' blood,
　　Where knelt the vanquished foe,
When winds were hurrying o'er the flood,
　　And waves were white below,
No more shall feel the victor's tread,
　　Or know the conquered knee;—
The harpies of the shore shall pluck
　　The eagle of the sea!

Oh, better that her shattered hulk
　　Should sink beneath the wave;
Her thunders shook the mighty deep,
　　And there should be her grave;
Nail to the mast her holy flag,
　　Set every threadbare sail,
And give her to the god of storms,
　　The lightning and the gale!

(Written in protest against the proposed
breaking up of the frigate *Constitution*)

[ 197 ]

# THE FIRST "MORGAN"

## Marguerite Henry

This is the story of a common ordinary little work horse which turned out to be the father of a famous family of American horses. He lived in the Green Mountain country of Vermont in the days when our country was growing up. In fact, he helped it grow up. He dragged logs and cleared the land. He helped build the first log huts. He helped build bridges and cut roads through the wilderness.

There was not much that this courageous little horse could not do. He labored hard by day. At the end of the day he took part in races and pulling bees. He could walk faster, trot faster, run faster, and pull heavier logs than any horse in Vermont.

Today his descendants, known as Morgan horses, are famous throughout the world. Yet nobody knows whether the first Morgan's parents were British or French or Dutch. And nobody really cares. As Joel Goss said, "Come to think of it, he's like us. He's American. That's what he is. American!"

—From *Justin Morgan Had a Horse*

## THE STAR-SPANGLED BANNER

Francis Scott Key

O say, can you see, by the dawn's early light,
What so proudly we hailed at the twilight's last gleaming?
Whose broad stripes and bright stars, through the perilous fight,
O'er the ramparts we watched were so gallantly streaming!
And the rockets' red glare, the bombs bursting in air,
Gave proof through the night that our flag was still there:
O say, does that star-spangled banner yet wave
O'er the land of the free and the home of the brave?

On the shore, dimly seen through the mists of the deep,
Where the foe's haughty host in dread silence reposes,
What is that which the breeze, o'er the towering steep,
As it fitfully blows, half conceals, half discloses?
Now it catches the gleam of the morning's first beam,
In full glory reflected now shines on the stream.
'Tis the star-spangled banner! O long may it wave
O'er the land of the free and the home of the brave!

And where is that band who so vauntingly swore
That the havoc of war and the battle's confusion

A home and a country should leave us no more?
Their blood has washed out their foul footsteps' pollution.
No refuge could save the hireling and slave
From the terror of flight, or the gloom of the grave:
And the star-spangled banner in triumph doth wave
O'er the land of the free and the home of the brave!

O thus be it ever, when freemen shall stand
Between their loved homes and the war's desolation!
Blest with victory and peace, may the heaven-rescued land
Praise the Power that hath made and preserved us a nation.
Then conquer we must, when our cause it is just,
And this be our motto: "In God is our trust,"
And the star-spangled banner in triumph shall wave
O'er the land of the free and the home of the brave!

—(Written during the bombardment of Fort McHenry, September 3, 1814)

## HENRY CLAY SAID

Sir, I would rather be right than be President.

# THE MONROE DOCTRINE

### James Monroe

The American continents . . . . are henceforth not to be considered as subjects for future colonization by any European powers. . . .

We owe it, therefore, to candor and to the amicable relations existing between the United States and those powers to declare that we should consider any attempt on their part to extend their system to any portion of this hemisphere as dangerous to our peace and safety.

With the existing colonies or dependencies of any European power we have not interfered and shall not interfere. But with the Governments who have declared their independence and maintained it, and whose independence we have, on great consideration and on just principles, acknowledged, we could not view any interposition for the purpose of oppressing them, or controlling in any other manner their destiny, by any European power, in any other light than as the manifestation of an unfriendly disposition toward the United States.

—From President James Monroe's annual message to Congress on December 2, 1823

# A LETTER FROM THE ALAMO

COMMANDANCY OF THE ALAMO, TEXAS
February 24, 1836

*To the People of Texas and All Americans in the World.*
FELLOW CITIZENS AND COMPATRIOTS:

I am besieged by a thousand or more of the Mexicans under Santa Anna. I have sustained a continual bombardment and cannonade for twenty-four hours and have not lost a man. The enemy has demanded a surrender at discretion; otherwise the garrison are to be put to the sword if the fort is taken. I have answered the demand with a cannon shot, and our flag still waves proudly from the walls. *I shall never surrender nor retreat.* Then, I call on you in the name of Liberty, of patriotism, and of everything dear to the American character, to come to our aid with all dispatch. The enemy is receiving reinforcements daily and will no doubt increase to three or four thousand in four or five days. If this call is neglected, I am determined to sustain myself as long as possible and die like a soldier who never forgets what is due to his own honor and that of his country.

VICTORY OR DEATH.

WILLIAM BARRET TRAVIS
*Lieutenant Colonel, Commandant*

(The siege of the Alamo continued until March 6th, when the garrison was overwhelmed by superior numbers of the enemy. The entire garrison, including Colonel Travis, James Bowie, David Crockett and nearly 150 others, lost their lives in its heroic defense.)

## MOTTO

### David Crockett

I leave this rule for others when I'm dead,
Be always sure you're right—then go ahead.

## GOD GRANTS LIBERTY

### Daniel Webster

God grants liberty only to those who love it, and are always
ready to guard and defend it.

## A LIFE ON THE OCEAN WAVE

Epes Sargent

A life on the ocean wave,
   A home on the rolling deep,
Where the scattered waters rave,
   And the winds their revels keep!
Like an eagle caged, I pine
   On this dull, unchanging shore:
Oh! give me the flashing brine,
   The spray and the tempest's roar!

—Selected from "A Life on the Ocean Wave"

## LET US BE OF GOOD CHEER

James Russell Lowell

Let us be of good cheer, however, remembering that the misfortunes hardest to bear are those which never come.

—From "Democracy"

## LOST . . . FOREVER
### Horace Mann

Lost, yesterday, somewhere between sunrise and sunset, two golden hours, each set with sixty diamond minutes. No reward is offered for they are gone forever.

## THE WILDERNESS IS TAMED
### Elizabeth J. Coatsworth

The axe has cut the forest down,
The laboring ox has smoothed all clear,
Apples now grow where pine trees stood,
And slow cows graze instead of deer.

Where Indian fires once raised their smoke
The chimneys of a farmhouse stand,
And cocks crow barnyard challenges
To dawns that once saw savage land.

The axe, the plow, the binding wall,
By these the wilderness is tamed,
By these the white man's will is wrought,
The rivers bridged, the new towns named.

# O MOTHER OF A MIGHTY RACE

William Cullen Bryant

O mother of a mighty race,
Yet lovely in thy youthful grace!
The elder dames, thy haughty peers,
Admire and hate thy blooming years.
 With words of shame
And taunts of scorn they join thy name.

For on thy cheeks the glow is spread
That tints thy morning hills with red;
Thy step—the wild deer's rustling feet
Within thy woods are not more fleet;
 Thy hopeful eye
Is bright as thine own sunny sky.

Ay, let them rail—those haughty ones,
While safe thou dwellest with thy sons.
They do not know how loved thou art,
How many a fond and fearless heart
 Would rise to throw
Its life between thee and the foe.

They know not, in their hate and pride,
What virtues with thy children bide;

How true, how good, thy graceful maids
Make bright, like flowers, the valley-shades;
   What generous men
Spring, like thine oaks, by hill and glen;—

What cordial welcomes greet the guest
By thy lone rivers of the West;
How faith is kept, and truth revered,
And man is loved, and God is feared,
   In woodland homes,
And where the ocean border foams.

There's freedom at thy gates and rest
For Earth's down-trodden and opprest,
A shelter for the hunted head,
For the starved laborer toil and bread.
   Power, at thy bounds,
Stops and calls back his baffled hounds.

Oh, fair young mother! on thy brow
Shall sit a nobler grace than now.
Deep in the brightness of the skies
The thronging years in glory rise,
   And, as they fleet,
Drop strength and riches at thy feet.

# THE OLD OAKEN BUCKET
Samuel Woodworth

How dear to this heart are the scenes of my childhood,
   When fond recollection presents them to view!
The orchard, the meadow, the deep-tangled wildwood,
   And every loved spot which my infancy knew;
The wide-spreading pond, and the mill that stood by it;
   The bridge and the rock where the cataract fell;
The cot of my father, the dairy-house nigh it,
   And e'en the rude bucket which hung in the well!
The old oaken bucket, the iron-bound bucket,
   The moss-covered bucket which hung in the well.

That moss-covered vessel I hail as a treasure;
   For often, at noon, when returned from the field,
I found it the source of an exquisite pleasure,
   The purest and sweetest that nature can yield.
How ardent I seized it, with hands that were glowing,
   And quick to the white-pebbled bottom it fell;
Then soon, with the emblem of truth overflowing,
   And dripping with coolness, it rose from the well;
The old oaken bucket, the iron-bound bucket,
   The moss-covered bucket arose from the well.

How sweet from the green mossy brim to receive it,
   As poised on the curb, it inclined to my lips!
Not a full blushing goblet could tempt me to leave it,

Though filled with the nectar which Jupiter sips;
And now, far removed from thy loved situation,
　　The tear of regret will intrusively swell,
As fancy reverts to my father's plantation,
　　And sighs for the bucket which hangs in the well;
The old oaken bucket, the iron-bound bucket,
　　The moss-covered bucket, which hangs in the well.

—Selected from "The Old Oaken Bucket"

## RICHES

### Henry David Thoreau

A man is rich in proportion to the number of things which he can afford to let alone.

—From Walden

## GO CONFIDENTLY!

### Henry David Thoreau

Go confidently in the direction of your dreams! Live the life you've imagined! As you simplify your life, the laws of the universe will be simpler, solitude will not be solitude, poverty will not be poverty, nor weakness weakness.

—Adapted from Walden

# OLD FOLKS AT HOME

Stephen Foster

'Way down upon de Swanee Ribber,
Far, far away,
Dere's wha' my heart is turning ebber,
Dere's wha' de old folks stay.
All up and down de whole creation
Sadly I roam,
Still longing for de old plantation,
And for de old folks at home.

*Chorus:*

All de world am sad and dreary,
Ebrywhere I roam;
Oh, darkies, how my heart grows weary,
Far from de old folks at home!

All round de little farm I wandered
When I was young,
Den many happy days I squandered
Many de songs I sung.
When I was playing wid my brudder
Happy was I;
Oh, take me to my kind old mudder!
Dere let me live and die.

One little hut among de bushes,
One dat I love,
Still sadly to my memory rushes,
No matter where I rove.
When will I see the bees a-humming
All round de comb?
When will I hear de banjo tumming,
Down in my good old home?

## MY OLD KENTUCKY HOME

Stephen Foster

The sun shines bright in the old Kentucky home;
  'Tis summer, the darkies are gay;
The corn top's ripe, and the meadow's in the bloom,
  While the birds make music all the day.
The young folks roll on the little cabin floor,
  All merry, all happy, and bright;
By-'n'-by hard times comes a knocking at the door:—
  Then my old Kentucky home, good night!

*Chorus:*

      Weep no more, my lady; Oh, weep no more today!
      We will sing one song for the old Kentucky home,
      For the old Kentucky home, far away.

They hunt no more for the possum and the coon,
  On the meadow, the hill, and the shore;
They sing no more by the glimmer of the moon,
  On the bench by the old cabin door.
The day goes by like a shadow o'er the heart,
  With sorrow, where all was delight;

The time has come when the darkies have to part:—
Then my old Kentucky home, good night!

The head must bow, and the back will have to bend,
Wherever the darky may go;
A few more days and the troubles all will end,
In the fields where the sugar-canes grow.
A few more days for to tote the weary load—
No matter, 'twill never be light;
A few more days till we totter on the road:—
Then my old Kentucky home, good night!

# I WENT TO THE WOODS

Henry David Thoreau

I went to the woods because I wished to live deliberately, to front only the essential facts of life, and see if I could not learn what it had to teach, and not, when I came to die, discover that I had not lived.

—From *Walden*

# SAYINGS OF
# RALPH WALDO EMERSON

### TO FIND THE BEAUTIFUL

Though we travel the world over to find the beautiful, we must carry it with us or we find it not.

—From "Art"

### THE WISDOM OF A MAN

Now that is the wisdom of a man, in every instance of his labor, to hitch his wagon to a star, and see his chore done by the gods themselves.

—From "Civilization"

### ENTHUSIASM

Nothing great was ever achieved without enthusiasm.

—From "Circles"

### EVERY GENUINE WORK OF ART

Every genuine work of art has as much reason for being as the earth and the sun.

—From "Art"

## LIBERTY AND UNION
### Daniel Webster

I profess, sir, in my career hitherto to have kept steadily in view the prosperity and honor of the whole country and the preservation of our Federal Union. It is to that Union we owe our safety at home, and our consideration and dignity abroad. It is to that Union that we are chiefly indebted for whatever makes us most proud of our country. That Union we reached only by the discipline of our virtues in the severe school of adversity. It had its origin in the necessities of disordered finance, prostrate commerce, and ruined credit. Under its benign influences these great interests immediately awoke, as from the dead, and sprang forth with newness of life. Every year of its duration has teemed with fresh proofs of its utility and its blessings; and although our territory has stretched out wider and wider, and our population spread farther and farther, they have not outrun its protection or its benefits. It has been to us all a copious fountain of national, social, and personal happiness.

\*     \*     \*

While the Union lasts we have high, exciting, gratifying prospects spread out before us, for us and our children. Beyond that I seek not to penetrate the veil. God grant that, in my day, at least, that curtain may not rise! God grant that on my vision never may be opened what lies behind! When my eyes shall be turned to behold for the last time the sun in heaven, may I not see him shining on the broken and dishonored fragments of a once glorious Union; on States dissevered, discordant, belligerent; on a land rent with civil feuds, or drenched, it may be, in fraternal blood! Let their last feeble and lingering glance rather behold the gorgeous ensign of the Republic, now known and honored throughout the earth, still full high advanced, its arms and trophies streaming in their original luster, not a stripe erased or polluted, nor a single star obscured, bearing for its motto no such miserable interrogatory as, "What is all this worth?" nor those other words of delusion and folly, "Liberty first and Union afterward"; but everywhere, spread all over in characters of living light, blazing on all its ample folds, as they float over the sea and over the land, and in every wind under the whole heavens, that other sentiment dear to every American heart—Liberty *and* Union, now and forever, one and inseparable!

—From the *Reply to Hayne*, 1830

## THE CONSTITUTION
### Salmon Portland Chase

The Constitution, in all its provisions, looks to an indestructible Union composed of indestructible States.

—From *Decision* in Texas vs. White

## THE BIBLE
### John Greenleaf Whittier

We search the world for truth; we cull
The good, the pure, the beautiful,
From graven stone and written scroll,
And all old flower-fields of the soul;
And, weary seekers of the best,
We come back laden from our quest,
To find that all the sages said
Is in the Book our mothers read,
And all our treasure of old thought
In His harmonious fullness wrought
Who gathers in one sheaf complete
The scattered blades of God's sown wheat,
The common growth that maketh good
His all-embracing Fatherhood.

—From "Miriam"

## OR MAKE A BETTER MOUSETRAP
### Attributed to Ralph Waldo Emerson

If a man can write a better book, preach a better sermon, or make a better mousetrap than his neighbors, though he builds his house in the woods, the world will make a beaten path to his door.

# BE NOBLE!

### James Russell Lowell

"For this true nobleness I seek in vain,
  In woman and in man I find it not;
  I almost weary of my earthly lot,
  My life-springs are dried up with burning pain."
Thou find'st it not? I pray thee look again,
  Look *inward* through the depths of thine own soul.
  How is it with thee? Art thou sound and whole?
  Doth narrow search show thee no earthly stain?
Be noble! and the nobleness that lies
  In other men, sleeping, but never dead,
  Will rise in majesty to meet thine own;
Then wilt thou see it gleam in many eyes,
  Then will pure light around thy path be shed,
  And thou wilt nevermore be sad and lone.

—From "Sonnets" IV

# THE AXIS OF THE EARTH

### Oliver Wendell Holmes

The axis of the earth sticks out visibly through the center of each and every town or city.

—From *The Autocrat of the Breakfast Table*

## A NATION'S STRENGTH

Ralph Waldo Emerson

Not gold, but only man can make
  A people great and strong;
Men who, for truth and honor's sake,
  Stand fast and suffer long.

Brave men who work while others sleep,
  Who dare while others fly—
They build a nation's pillars deep
  And lift them to the sky.


## WENDELL PHILLIPS SAID

One on God's side is a majority.

\*   \*   \*

Eternal vigilance is the price of liberty.

## SAIL ON, O SHIP OF STATE!

### Henry Wadsworth Longfellow

Thou, too, sail on, O Ship of State!
Sail on, O Union, strong and great!
Humanity with all its fears,
With all its hopes of future years,
Is hanging breathless on thy fate!
We know what Master laid thy keel,
What Workmen wrought thy ribs of steel,
Who made each mast, and sail, and rope,
What anvils rang, what hammers beat,
In what a forge and what a heat
Were shaped the anchors of thy hope!
Fear not each sudden sound and shock,
'Tis of the wave and not the rock;
'Tis but the flapping of the sail,
And not a rent made by a gale!
In spite of rock and tempest's roar,
In spite of false lights on the shore,
Sail on, nor fear to breast the sea!
Our hearts, our hopes, are all with thee,
Our hearts, our hopes, our prayers, our tears,
Our faith, triumphant o'er our fears,
Are all with thee,—are all with thee!

—From "The Building of the Ship"

## THEY ARE SLAVES WHO FEAR

### James Russell Lowell

They are slaves who fear to speak
For the fallen and the weak;
They are slaves who will not choose
Hatred, scoffing, and abuse,
Rather than in silence shrink
From the truth they needs must think;
They are slaves who dare not be
In the right with two or three.

—From "Stanzas on Freedom"

## THE DAY'S DEMAND

### Josiah Gilbert Holland

God give us men! A time like this demands
  Strong minds, great hearts, true faith, and
    ready hands;
Men whom the lust of office does not kill;
  Men whom the spoils of office cannot buy;
Men who possess opinions and a will;
  Men who have honor; men who will not lie!

—From "Wanted"

# ONCE TO EVERY MAN AND NATION

### James Russell Lowell

. . . Once to every man and nation comes the
     moment to decide,
In the strife of Truth with Falsehood, for
     the good or evil side;
Some great cause, God's new Messiah, offering
     each the bloom or blight,
Parts the goats upon the left hand, and the
     sheep upon the right,
And the choice goes by for ever 'twixt that
     darkness and that light.

Hast thou chosen, O my people, on whose
     party thou shalt stand,
Ere the Doom from its worn sandals shakes
     the dust against our land?
Though the cause of Evil prosper, yet 'tis
     Truth alone is strong,
And, albeit she wander outcast now, I see
     around her throng
Troops of beautiful, tall angels, to enshield
     her from all wrong.

Careless seems the great Avenger; history's
     pages but record
One death-grapple in the darkness 'twixt
     old systems and the Word;
Truth forever on the scaffold, Wrong for-
     ever on the throne—
Yet that scaffold sways the future, and be-
     hind the dim unknown,
Standeth God within the shadow, keeping
     watch above his own.

Then to side with Truth is noble when we
    share her wretched crust,
Ere her cause bring fame and profit, and
    'tis prosperous to be just;
Then it is the brave man chooses, while
    the coward stands aside,
Doubting in his abject spirit, till his Lord
    is crucified,
And the multitude make virtue of the faith
    they had denied.

New occasions teach new duties; Time makes
    ancient good uncouth;
They must upward still, and onward, who
    would keep abreast of Truth;
Lo! before us gleam her camp-fires! we
    ourselves must Pilgrims be,
Launch our Mayflower, and steer boldly
    through the desperate winter sea,
Nor attempt the Future's portal with the
    Past's blood-rusted key.

—From "The Present Crisis"

## THE ARSENAL AT SPRINGFIELD

Henry Wadsworth Longfellow

Were half the power that fills the world with terror,
Were half the wealth bestowed on camps and courts,
Given to redeem the human mind from error,
There were no need of arsenals or forts.

—Selected from "The Arsenal at Springfield"

## THE ETERNAL STRUGGLE
### Abraham Lincoln

. . . It is the eternal struggle between these two principles—right and wrong—throughout the world. They are the two principles that have stood face to face from the beginning of time and will ever continue to struggle. The one is the common right of humanity, and the other the divine right of kings. It is the same principle in whatever shape it develops itself. It is the same spirit that says, "You toil and work and earn bread, and I will eat it." No matter in what shape it comes, whether from the mouth of a king who seeks to bestride the people of his own nation and live from the fruit of their labor, or from one race of men as an apology for enslaving another race, it is the same tyrannical principle.

—From *The Lincoln-Douglas Debates (1858)*


## OUR COUNTRY, RIGHT OR WRONG
### Carl Schurz

Our country, right or wrong. When right, to be kept right; when wrong, to be put right.

## SAYINGS OF ABRAHAM LINCOLN

It is difficult to make a man miserable while he feels he is worthy of himself and claims kindred to the great God who made him.

\* \* \*

Let us have faith that right makes might, and in that faith let us to the end dare to do our duty as we understand it.

\* \* \*

I am not bound to win, but I am bound to be true. I am not bound to succeed, but I am bound to live up to what light I have. I must stand with anybody that stands right, stand with him while he is right, and part with him when he goes wrong.

\* \* \*

I do the very best I know how—the very best I can; and I mean to keep doing so until the end. If the end brings me out all right, what is said against me won't amount to anything. If the end brings me out wrong, ten thousand angels swearing I was right would make no difference.

\* \* \*

If we do not make common cause to save the good old ship of the Union on this voyage, nobody will have a chance to pilot her on another voyage.

\* \* \*

A house divided against itself cannot stand. I believe this government cannot endure permanently half slave and half free.

\* \* \*

Our reliance is in the love of liberty which God has planted in us. Our defense is in the spirit which prizes liberty as the heritage of all men, in all lands everywhere.

\* \* \*

As I would not be a slave, so I would not be a master. This expresses my idea of democracy. Whatever differs from this, to the extent of the difference, is no democracy.

\* \* \*

If you call a tail a leg, how many legs has a dog? Five? No; calling a tail a leg doesn't *make* it a leg.

\* \* \*

You can fool some of the people all of the time and all of the people some of the time: but you can't fool all the people all of the time.

\* \* \*

I have not allowed myself to suppose that I am the greatest or best man in America; but I am reminded in this connection of a story of an old Dutch farmer, who remarked to a companion once that it was not best to swap horses when crossing a stream.

## NANCY HANKS

Rosemary Benét

If Nancy Hanks
Came back as a ghost,
Seeking news
Of what she loved most,
She'd ask first,
"Where's my son?
What's happened to Abe?
What's he done?

"Poor little Abe,
Left all alone
Except for Tom,
Who's a rolling stone;
He was only nine
The year I died.
I remember still
How hard he cried.

"Scraping along
In a little shack,
With hardly a shirt
To cover his back,
And a prairie wind
To blow him down,
Or pinching times
If he went to town.

"You wouldn't know
   About my son?
   Did he grow tall?
   Did he have fun?
   Did he learn to read?
   Did he get to town?
   Do you know his name?
   Did he get on?"

## DIXIE

### Daniel Decatur Emmett

I wish I was in de land ob cotton,
Old times dar am not forgotten;
   Look away, look away, look away, Dixie land!
In Dixie land whar I was born in,
Early on one frosty mornin',
   Look away, look away, look away, Dixie land!

*Chorus:*
   Den I wish I was in Dixie! Hooray! Hooray!
   In Dixie's land we'll take our stand,
      to lib an' die in Dixie,
   Away, away, away down south in Dixie!
   Away, away, away down south in Dixie!

Dis world was made in jis' six days,
An' finished up in various ways.
    Look away! look away! look away! Dixie land!
Dey den make Dixie trim and nice,
And Adam called it "Paradise."
    Look away! look away! look away! Dixie land!

Dar's buckwheat cakes and Injun batter,
Makes you fat er a little fatter;
    Look away, look away, look away, Dixie land!
Den hoe it down an' scratch your grabbel,
To Dixie's land I'm bound to trabbel;
    Look away, look away, look away, Dixie land!

—Selected from "Dixie"

## CHRISTMAS BELLS

Henry Wadsworth Longfellow

I heard the bells on Christmas Day
Their old, familiar carols play,
    And wild and sweet
    The words repeat
Of peace on earth, good-will to men!

And thought how, as the day had come,
The belfries of all Christendom
    Had rolled along
    The unbroken song
Of peace on earth, good-will to men!

[ 228 ]

Till, ringing, singing on its way,
The world revolved from night to day,
    A voice, a chime,
    A chant sublime
Of peace on earth, good-will to men!

Then from each black, accursed mouth
The cannon thundered in the South,
    And with the sound
    The carols drowned
Of peace on earth, good-will to men!

It was as if an earthquake rent
The hearth-stones of a continent,
    And made forlorn
    The households born
Of peace on earth, good-will to men!

And in despair I bowed my head;
"There is no peace on earth," I said;
    "For hate is strong,
    And mocks the song
Of peace on earth, good-will to men!"

Then pealed the bells more loud and deep:
"God is not dead; nor doth He sleep!
    The Wrong shall fail,
    The Right prevail,
With peace on earth, good-will to men!"

# BATTLE-HYMN OF THE REPUBLIC
## Julia Ward Howe

Mine eyes have seen the glory of the coming of the Lord;
He is trampling out the vintage where the grapes of wrath are
    stored;
He hath loosed the fateful lightning of His terrible swift sword;
        His truth is marching on.

I have seen Him in the watch-fires of a hundred circling camps;
They have builded Him an altar in the evening dews and damps;
I can read His righteous sentence by the dim and flaring lamps;
        His day is marching on.

I have read a fiery gospel, writ in burnished rows of steel:
"As ye deal with my contemners, so with you my grace shall deal;
Let the Hero, born of woman, crush the serpent with his heel,
        Since God is marching on."

He has sounded forth the trumpet that shall never call retreat;
He is sifting out the hearts of men before His judgment-seat:
Oh, be swift, my soul, to answer Him! be jubilant my feet!
    Our God is marching on.

In the beauty of the lilies Christ was born across the sea,
With a glory in His bosom that transfigures you and me;
As he died to make men holy, let us die to make men free,
        While God is marching on.

# THREE HUNDRED THOUSAND MORE

### James Sloane Gibbons

We are coming, Father Abraham, three hundred thousand more,
From Mississippi's winding stream and from New England's shore;
We leave our plows and workshops, our wives and children dear,
With hearts too full for utterance, with but a silent tear;
We dare not look behind us, but steadfastly before;
We are coming, Father Abraham, three hundred thousand more!

If you look across the hilltops that meet the northern sky,
Long moving lines of rising dust your vision may descry;
And now the wind, an instant, tears the cloudy veil aside,
And floats aloft our spangled flag, in glory and in pride,
And bayonets in the sunlight gleam, and bands brave music pour;
We are coming, Father Abraham, three hundred thousand more!

If you look all up our valleys where the growing harvests shine,
You may see our sturdy farmer boys fast forming into line;
And children from their mothers' knees are pulling at the weeds,
And learning how to reap and sow against their country's needs.
And a farewell group stands weeping at every cottage door;
We are coming, Father Abraham, three hundred thousand more!

## BARBARA FRIETCHIE

John Greenleaf Whittier

Up from the meadows rich with corn,
Clear in the cool September morn,

The clustered spires of Frederick stand
Green-walled by the hills of Maryland.

Round about them orchards sweep,
Apple and peach-tree fruited deep,

Fair as a garden of the Lord
To the eyes of the famished rebel horde,

On that pleasant morn of the early fall
When Lee marched over the mountain wall;

Over the mountains winding down,
Horse and foot, into Frederick town.

Forty flags with their silver stars,
Forty flags with their crimson bars,

Flapped in the morning wind: the sun
Of noon looked down, and saw not one.

Up rose old Barbara Frietchie then,
Bowed with her fourscore years and ten;

Bravest of all in Frederick town,
She took up the flag the men hauled down;

In her attic window the staff she set,
To show that one heart was loyal yet.

Up the street came the rebel tread,
Stonewall Jackson riding ahead.

Under his slouched hat left and right
He glanced; the old flag met his sight.

"Halt!"—the dust-brown ranks stood fast.
"Fire!"—out blazed the rifle blast.

It shivered the window, pane and sash;
It rent the banner with seam and gash.

Quick, as it fell, from the broken staff
Dame Barbara snatched the silken scarf.

She leaned far out on the window-sill,
And shook it forth with a royal will.

"Shoot, if you must, this old gray head,
But spare your country's flag," she said.

A shade of sadness, a blush of shame,
Over the face of the leader came;

The nobler nature within him stirred
To life at the woman's deed and word;

"Who touches a hair of yon gray head
Dies like a dog! March on!" he said.

All day long through Frederick street
Sounded the tread of marching feet:

All day long that free flag tost
Over the heads of the rebel host.

Ever its torn folds rose and fell
On the loyal winds that loved it well;

And through the hill-gaps sunset light
Shone over it with a warm good-night.

Barbara Frietchie's work is o'er,
And the Rebel rides on his raids no more.

Honor to her! and let a tear
Fall, for her sake, on Stonewall's bier.

Over Barbara Frietchie's grave,
Flag of Freedom and Union, wave!

Peace and order and beauty draw
Round thy symbol of light and law;

And ever the stars above look down
On thy stars below in Frederick town!

## SHERIDAN'S RIDE

### Thomas Buchanan Read

Up from the South, at break of day,
Bringing to Winchester fresh dismay,
   The affrighted air with a shudder bore,
   Like a herald in haste, to the chieftain's door,
   The terrible grumble, and rumble, and roar,
   Telling the battle was on once more,
And Sheridan twenty miles away.

And wider still those billows of war
Thundered along the horizon's bar;
And louder yet into Winchester rolled
The roar of that red sea uncontrolled,
Making the blood of the listener cold,
As he thought of the stake in that fiery fray,
And Sheridan twenty miles away.

But there is a road from Winchester town,
A good, broad highway leading down;

And there, through the flush of the morning light,
A steed as black as the steeds of night
Was seen to pass, as with eagle flight,
As if he knew the terrible need;
He stretched away with his utmost speed;
Hills rose and fell; but his heart was gay,
With Sheridan fifteen miles away.

Still sprung from those swift hoofs, thundering South,
The dust, like smoke from the cannon's mouth;
Or the trail of a comet, sweeping faster and faster,
Foreboding to traitors the doom of disaster.
The heart of the steed and the heart of the master
Were beating like prisoners assaulting their walls,
Impatient to be where the battlefield calls;
Every nerve of the charger was trained to full play,
With Sheridan only ten miles away.

Under his spurning feet the road
Like an arrowy Alpine river flowed,
And the landscape sped away behind
Like an ocean flying before the wind,
And the steed, like a bark fed with furnace ire,
Swept on, with his wild eye full of fire.
But lo! he is nearing his heart's desire;
He is snuffing the smoke of the roaring fray,
With Sheridan only five miles away.

The first that the general saw were the groups
Of stragglers, and then the retreating troops.
What was done? What to do? A glance told him both.
Then striking his spurs, with a terrible oath,
He dashed down the line, 'mid a storm of huzzas,
And the wave of retreat checked its course there, because
The sight of the master compelled it to pause.

With foam and with dust, the black charger was gray;
By the flash of his eye, and red nostril's play,
He seemed to the whole great army to say:
"I have brought you Sheridan all the way
From Winchester town to save the day!"

Hurrah! Hurrah for Sheridan!
Hurrah! Hurrah for horse and man!
And when their statues are placed on high,
Under the dome of the Union sky,
The American soldiers' Temple of Fame;
There, with the glorious general's name,
Be it said, in letters both bold and bright:
"Here is the steed that saved the day,
By carrying Sheridan into the fight,
From Winchester—twenty miles away!"

# THE GETTYSBURG ADDRESS

## Abraham Lincoln

Fourscore and seven years ago our fathers brought forth upon this continent a new nation, conceived in liberty, and dedicated to the proposition that all men are created equal. Now we are engaged in a great civil war, testing whether that nation, or any nation so conceived and so dedicated, can long endure. We are met on a great battlefield of that war. We have come to dedicate a portion of that field as a final resting place for those who here gave their lives that that nation might live. It is altogether fitting and proper that we should do this. But in a larger sense we cannot dedicate, we cannot consecrate, we cannot hallow this ground. The brave men, living and dead, who struggled here, have consecrated it far above our poor power to add or detract. The world will little note, nor long remember, what we say here; but it can never forget what they did here. It is for us, the living, rather to be dedicated here to the unfinished work which they who fought here have thus far so nobly advanced. It is rather for us to be here dedicated to the great task remaining before us, that from these honored dead we take increased devotion to that cause for which they gave the last full measure of devotion; that we here highly resolve that these dead shall not have died in vain; that this nation, under God, shall have a new birth of freedom, and that government of the people, by the people, and for the people, shall not perish from the earth.

—Delivered at Gettysburg, Pennsylvania, November 19, 1863

# ABRAHAM LINCOLN'S LETTER
## TO MRS. BIXBY

November 21, 1864

DEAR MADAM:

I have been shown in the files of the War Department a statement of the Adjutant-General of Massachusetts that you are the mother of five sons who have died gloriously on the field of battle. I feel how weak and fruitless must be any words of mine which should attempt to beguile you from the grief of a loss so overwhelming. But I cannot refrain from tendering to you the consolation that may be found in the thanks of the Republic that they died to save. I pray that our Heavenly Father may assuage the anguish of your bereavement, and leave you only the cherished memory of the loved and lost, and the solemn pride that must be yours to have laid so costly a sacrifice upon the altar of freedom.

Yours very sincerely and respectfully,

ABRAHAM LINCOLN

# FROM THE
# SECOND INAUGURAL ADDRESS
### Abraham Lincoln

With malice toward none; with charity for all; with firmness in the right, as God gives us to see the right, let us strive on to finish the work we are in; to bind up the nation's wounds; to care for him who shall have borne the battle, and for his widow and his orphan—to do all which may achieve and cherish a just and lasting peace among ourselves and with all nations.

—Delivered on March 4, 1865

# ROBERT E. LEE'S
# FAREWELL TO HIS ARMY

## HEADQUARTERS ARMY OF NORTHERN VIRGINIA

### April 10, 1865

After four years of arduous service, marked by unsurpassed courage and fortitude, the Army of Northern Virginia has been compelled to yield to overwhelming numbers and resources.

I need not tell the survivors of so many hard-fought battles, who have remained steadfast to the last, that I have consented to this result from no distrust of them; but, feeling that valor and devotion could accomplish nothing that could compensate for the loss that would have attended the continuation of the contest, I have determined to avoid the useless sacrifice of those whose past services have endeared them to their countrymen.

By the terms of the agreement, officers and men can return to their homes and remain until exchanged.

You may take with you the satisfaction that proceeds from the consciousness of duty faithfully performed, and I earnestly pray that a merciful God will extend to you His blessing and protection.

With an unceasing admiration of your constancy and devotion to your country, and a grateful remembrance of your kind and generous consideration of myself, I bid you all an affectionate farewell.

R. E. LEE, *General*

## WAR

### William Tecumseh Sherman

I am tired and sick of war. Its glory is all moonshine. It is only those who have neither fired a shot nor heard the shrieks and groans of the wounded who cry aloud for blood, more vengeance, more desolation. War is hell.

## TRUTH, THE INVINCIBLE

### William Cullen Bryant

Truth, crushed to earth, shall rise again;
 The eternal years of God are hers;
But Error, wounded, writhes in pain,
 And dies among his worshipers.

—From "The Battle-Field"

# O CAPTAIN! MY CAPTAIN!

### Walt Whitman

O Captain! my Captain! our fearful trip is done;
The ship has weather'd every rack, the prize we sought is won;
The port is near, the bells I hear, the people all exulting,
While follow eyes the steady keel, the vessel grim and daring:
    But O heart! heart! heart!
      O the bleeding drops of red,
        Where on the deck my Captain lies,
        Fallen cold and dead.

O Captain! my Captain! rise up and hear the bells;
Rise up—for you the flag is flung—for you the bugle trills;
For you bouquets and ribbon'd wreaths—for you the shores
  a-crowding;
For you they call, the swaying mass, their eager faces turning:
    Here Captain! dear father!
      This arm beneath your head!
        It is some dream that on the deck,
        You've fallen cold and dead.

My Captain does not answer, his lips are pale and still;
My father does not feel my arm, he has no pulse nor will;
The ship is anchor'd safe and sound, its voyage closed and done;
From fearful trip, the victor ship comes in with object won:
    Exult, O shores, and ring, O bells!
      But I, with mournful tread,
        Walk the deck my Captain lies,
        Fallen cold and dead.

## WHEN JOHNNY COMES MARCHING HOME

Patrick S. Gilmore

When Johnny comes marching home again,
Hurrah! Hurrah!
We'll give him a hearty welcome then,
Hurrah! Hurrah!
The men will cheer, the boys will shout,
The ladies they will all turn out,
And we'll all feel gay
When Johnny comes marching home.

The old church bell will peal with joy,
Hurrah! Hurrah!
To welcome home our darling boy,
Hurrah! Hurrah!
The village lads and lassies say
With roses they will strew the way,
And we'll all feel gay
When Johnny comes marching home.

Get ready for the Jubilee,
Hurrah! Hurrah!
We'll give the hero three times three,

[ 243 ]

Hurrah! Hurrah!
The laurel wreath is ready now
To place upon his loyal brow,
And we'll all feel gay
When Johnny comes marching home.

In eighteen hundred and sixty-one,
Hurrah! Hurrah!
That was when the war begun,
Hurrah! Hurrah!
In eighteen hundred and sixty-two,
Both sides were falling to;
And we'll all drink some wine
When Johnny comes marching home.

In eighteen hundred and sixty-four,
Hurrah! Hurrah!
Abe called for five hundred thousand more,
Hurrah! Hurrah!
In eighteen hundred and sixty-five,
They talked rebellion—strife;
And we'll all drink some wine
When Johnny comes marching home.

## THE BLUE AND THE GRAY

Francis Miles Finch

By the flow of the inland river,
  Whence the fleets of iron have fled,
Where the blades of the grave-grass quiver,
  Asleep are the ranks of the dead:—
Under the sod and the dew,
  Waiting the Judgment Day:—
Under the one, the Blue;
  Under the other, the Gray.

These in the robings of glory,
  Those in the gloom of defeat,
All with the battle-blood gory,
  In the dusk of eternity meet:—
Under the sod and the dew,
  Waiting the Judgment Day:—
Under the laurel, the Blue;
  Under the willow, the Gray.

From the silence of sorrowful hours
  The desolate mourners go,
Lovingly laden with flowers,
  Alike for the friend and the foe:—

Under the sod and the dew,
    Waiting the Judgment Day:—
Under the roses, the Blue;
    Under the lilies, the Gray.

So, with an equal splendor
    The morning sun-rays fall,
With a touch impartially tender,
    On the blossoms blooming for all:—
Under the sod and the dew,
    Waiting the Judgment Day:—
Broidered with gold, the Blue;
    Mellowed with gold, the Gray.

So, when the summer calleth,
    On forest and field of grain,
With an equal murmur falleth
    The cooling drip of the rain:—
Under the sod and the dew,
    Waiting the Judgment Day:—
Wet with the rain, the Blue;
    Wet with the rain, the Gray.

Sadly, but not with upbraiding,
    The generous deed was done.
In the storm of the years that are fading
    No braver battle was won:—
Under the sod and the dew,
    Waiting the Judgment Day;
Under the blossoms, the Blue;
    Under the garlands, the Gray.

No more shall the war cry sever,
    Or the winding rivers be red:
They banish our anger forever

When they laurel the graves of our dead!
Under the sod and the dew,
    Waiting the Judgment Day:—
Love and tears for the Blue;
    Tears and love for the Gray.

## THE NATIONAL FLAG

Charles Sumner

There is the National flag. He must be cold, indeed, who can look upon its folds rippling in the breeze without pride of country. If he be in a foreign land, the flag is companionship and country itself, with all its endearment. . . .

The very colors have a language which was officially recognized by our fathers. White is for purity; red, for valor; blue, for justice. And altogether, bunting, stripes, stars, and colors, blazing in the sky, make the flag of our country, to be cherished by all our hearts, to be upheld by all our hands.

—From *Are We a Nation?*

## I AM AN AMERICAN

### Elias Lieberman

I am an American.
My father belongs to the Sons of the Revolution;
My mother, to the Colonial Dames.
One of my ancestors pitched tea overboard in
    Boston Harbor;
Another stood his ground with Warren;
Another hungered with Washington at Valley Forge.
My forefathers were America in the making:
They spoke in her council halls;
They died on her battle-fields;
They commanded her ships;
They cleared her forests.
Dawns reddened and paled.
Staunch hearts of mine beat fast at each new star
In the nation's flag.
Keen eyes of mine foresaw her greater glory:
The sweep of her seas,
The plenty of her plains,
The man-hives in her billion-wired cities.

Every drop of blood in me holds a heritage of
    patriotism.
I am proud of my past.
I am an AMERICAN.

I am an American.
My father was an atom of dust,
My mother a straw in the wind,
To His Serene Majesty.
One of my ancestors died in the mines of Siberia;
Another was crippled for life by twenty blows of
    the knout.
Another was killed defending his home during the
    massacres.
The history of my ancestors is a trail of blood
To the palace-gate of the Great White Czar.
But then the dream came—
The dream of America.
In the light of the Liberty torch
The atom of dust became a man
And the straw in the wind became a woman
For the first time.
"See," said my father, pointing to the flag that
    fluttered near,
"That flag of stars and stripes is yours;
It is the emblem of the promised land.
It means, my son, the hope of humanity.
Live for it—die for it!"
Under the open sky of my new country I swore to do so;
And every drop of blood in me will keep that vow.
I am proud of my future.
I am an AMERICAN.

## THE STEADY GAIN OF MAN

John Greenleaf Whittier

Yet, sometimes glimpses on my sight,
Through present wrong, the eternal right;
And, step by step, since time began,
I see the steady gain of man;

That all of good the past hath had
Remains to make our own time glad,
Our common daily life divine,
And every land a Palestine.

We lack but open eye and ear
To find the Orient's marvels here;
The still small voice in autumn's hush,
Yon maple wood the burning bush.

For still the new transcends the old,
In signs and tokens manifold;
Slaves rise up men; the olive waves,
With roots deep set in battle graves!

Through the harsh voices of our day
A low, sweet prelude finds its way;
Through clouds of doubt, and creeds of fear,
A light is breaking, calm and clear.

—From "The Chapel of the Hermit"

## JUDGE NOT

### Joaquin Miller

In men whom men condemn as ill
I find so much of goodness still,
In men whom men pronounce divine
    I find so much of sin and blot,
I do not dare to draw a line
    Between the two, where God has not.

            —From "Byron"

## BOSTON

### Anonymous

I come from the city of Boston,
The home of the bean and the cod,
Where the Cabots speak only to Lowells,
And the Lowells speak only to God.

## TO ACHIEVE GREATNESS

### Walt Whitman

He or she is greatest who contributes the greatest original practical example.

            —From "By Blue Ontario's Shore"

# I HEAR AMERICA SINGING

### Walt Whitman

I hear America singing, the varied carols I hear;
Those of mechanics—each one singing his, as it should be, blithe and
    strong;
The carpenter singing his, as he measures his plank or beam,
The mason singing his, as he makes ready for work, or leaves off
    work;
The boatman singing what belongs to him in his boat—the deckhand
    singing on the steamboat deck;
The shoemaker singing as he sits on his bench—the hatter singing as
    he stands;
The wood-cutter's song—the ploughboy's on his way in the
    morning, or at noon intermission, or at sundown;
The delicious singing of the mother—or of the young wife at work
    —or of the girl sewing or washing—
Each singing what belongs to her and to none else;
The day what belongs to the day—at night, the party of young
    fellows, robust, friendly,
Singing, with open mouths, their strong melodious songs.

# THE GREAT MELTING POT

### Israel Zangwill

America is God's Crucible, the great Melting Pot where all the
races of Europe are melting and reforming! . . . God is making the
American.

—From *The Melting Pot*

## SO WHEN A GREAT MAN DIES

### Henry Wadsworth Longfellow

Were a star quenched on high,
For ages would its light,
Still traveling downward from the sky,
Shine on our mortal sight.

So when a great man dies,
For years beyond our ken,
The light he leaves behind him lies
Upon the paths of men.

—From "Charles Sumner"

## I'VE BEEN WORKIN' ON THE RAILROAD

### Anonymous

I've been workin' on the railroad
All the livelong day.
I've been workin' on the railroad
Just to pass the time away.
Don't you hear the whistle blowing?
Rise up so early in the morn.
Don't you hear the Captain shouting:
"Dinah, blow your horn."

## GO WEST, YOUNG MAN!

### Horace Greeley

The best business you can go into you will find on your father's farm or in his workshop. If you have no family or friends to aid you, and no prospect opened to you there, turn your face to the great West, and there build up a home and fortune.

## HOME ON THE RANGE

### Anonymous

O give me a home where the buffalo roam,
Where the deer and the antelope play,
Where seldom is heard a discouraging word
And the skies are not cloudy all day.

*Chorus:*
　　Home, home on the range,
　　Where the deer and the antelope play,
　　Where seldom is heard a discouraging word
　　And the skies are not cloudy all day.

## OUT WHERE THE WEST BEGINS

Arthur Chapman

Out where the handclasp's a little stronger,
Out where the smile dwells a little longer,
　That's where the West begins;
Out where the sun is a little brighter,
Where the snows that fall are a trifle whiter,
Where the bonds of home are a wee bit tighter,
　That's where the West begins.

Out where the skies are a trifle bluer,
Out where friendship's a little truer,
　That's where the West begins;
Out where a fresher breeze is blowing,
Where there's laughter in every streamlet flowing,
Where there's more of reaping and less of sowing,
　That's where the West begins.

Out where the world is in the making,
Where fewer hearts in despair are aching,
　That's where the West begins;
Where there's more of singing and less of sighing,
Where there's more of giving and less of buying,
And a man makes friends without half trying—
　That's where the West begins.

# BURY ME NOT ON THE LONE PRAIRIE

### Anonymous

"O bury me not on the lone prairie!"
These words came low and mournfully
From the pallid lips of a youth who lay
On his dying bed at the close of day.

"O bury me not on the lone prairie,
Where the wild coyotes will howl o'er me,
Where the buzzards beat and the wind goes free;
O bury me not on the lone prairie!

"O bury me not on the lone prairie,
In a narrow grave six foot by three,
Where the buffalo paws o'er a prairie sea;
O bury me not on the lone prairie!

"O bury me not on the lone prairie,
Where the wild coyotes will howl o'er me,
Where the rattlesnakes hiss and the crow flies free;
O bury me not on the lone prairie!

"O bury me not," and his voice faltered there,
But we took no heed of his dying prayer;
In a narrow grave just six by three
We buried him there on the lone prairie.

## WISDOM

James Russell Lowell

The wisest man could ask no more of Fate
Than to be simple, modest, manly, true,
Safe from the Many, honored by the Few;
To count as naught in World, or Church, or State;
But inwardly in secret to be great.

—From "Jeffries Wyman"

## MIRACLES

### Walt Whitman

Why, who makes much of a miracle?
As to me, I know of nothing else but miracles,
Whether I walk the streets of Manhattan,
Or dart my sight over the roofs of houses toward the sky,
Or wade with naked feet along the beach just in the edge of
      the water,
Or stand under trees in the woods,
Or talk by day with anyone I love, or sleep in the bed at
      night with anyone I love,
Or sit at table at dinner with the rest,
Or look at strangers opposite me riding in the car,
Or watch honeybees busy around the hive of a summer forenoon,
Or animals feeding in the fields,
Or birds, or the wonderfulness of insects in the air,
Or the wonderfulness of the sundown, or of stars shining so
      quiet and bright,
Or the exquisite delicate curve of the new moon in spring;
These with the rest, one and all, are to me miracles,
The whole referring, yet each distinct and in its place.
To me every hour of the light and dark is a miracle,
Every cubic inch of space is a miracle,

Every square yard of the surface of the earth is spread with
    the same,
Every foot of the interior swarms with the same.
To me the sea is a continual miracle,
The fishes that swim—the rocks—the motion of the
    waves—the ships with men in them,
What stranger miracles are there?

## POETRY

### Emily Dickinson

If I read a book and it makes my whole body so cold no fire can
ever warm me, I know that is poetry. If I feel physically as if the
top of my head were taken off, I know that is poetry. These are the
only ways I know it. Is there any other way?

                              —From *Life and Letters of Emily Dickinson*

# IN OURSELVES

Henry Wadsworth Longfellow

Not in the clamor of the crowded street,
Not in the shouts and plaudits of the throng,
But in ourselves, are triumph and defeat.

—From "The Poets"

# THE HANDS OF TOIL

James Russell Lowell

No man is born into the world whose work
Is not born with him; there is always work,
And tools to work withal, for those who will;
And blessed are the horny hands of toil.

—From "A Glance Behind the Curtain"

# AMERICA FOR ME
### Henry van Dyke

'Tis fine to see the Old World, and travel up and down
Among the famous palaces and cities of renown,
To admire the crumbly castles and the statues of the kings—
But now I think I've had enough of antiquated things.

So it's home again, and home again, America for me!
My heart is turning home again, and there I long to be,
In the land of youth and freedom beyond the ocean bars,
Where the air is full of sunlight and the flag is full of stars.

Oh, London is a man's town, there's power in the air;
And Paris is a woman's town, with flowers in her hair;
And it's sweet to dream in Venice, and it's great to study Rome;
But when it comes to living there is no place like home.

I like the German fir-woods, in green battalions drilled;
I like the gardens of Versailles, with dashing fountains filled;
But, oh, to take your hand, my dear, and ramble for a day
In the friendly western woodland where Nature has her way!

I know that Europe's wonderful, yet something seems to lack:
The Past is too much with her, and the people looking back.
But the glory of the Present is to make the Future free—
We love our land for what she is and what she is to be.

Oh, it's home again, and home again, America for me!
I want a ship that's westward bound to plough the rolling sea,
To the blessed Land of Room Enough beyond the ocean bars,
Where the air is full of sunshine and the flag is full of stars.

## THE VILLAGE BLACKSMITH
### Henry Wadsworth Longfellow

Under a spreading chestnut-tree
The village smithy stands;
The smith, a mighty man is he,
With large and sinewy hands;
And the muscles of his brawny arms
Are strong as iron bands.

His hair is crisp, and black, and long,
His face is like the tan;
His brow is wet with honest sweat,
He earns whate'er he can,
And looks the whole world in the face,
For he owes not any man.

Week in, week out, from morn till night,
You can hear his bellows blow;
You can hear him swing his heavy sledge,
With measured beat and slow,
Like a sexton ringing the village bell,
When the evening sun is low.

And children coming home from school
Look in at the open door;
They love to see the flaming forge,
And hear the bellows roar,
And catch the burning sparks that fly
Like chaff from a threshing-floor.

He goes on Sunday to the church,
And sits among his boys;
He hears the parson pray and preach,
He hears his daughter's voice,
Singing in the village choir,
And it makes his heart rejoice.

It sounds to him like her mother's voice,
Singing in Paradise!
He needs must think of her once more,
How in the grave she lies;
And with his hard, rough hand he wipes
A tear out of his eyes.

Toiling—rejoicing—sorrowing,
Onward through life he goes;
Each morning sees some task begin,
Each evening sees it close;
Something attempted, something done,
Has earned a night's repose.

Thanks, thanks to thee, my worthy friend,
For the lesson thou has taught!
Thus at the flaming forge of life
Our fortunes must be wrought;
Thus on its sounding anvil shaped
Each burning deed and thought!

## THE NEW COLOSSUS

Emma Lazarus

Not like the brazen giant of Greek fame,
With conquering limbs astride from land to land;
Here at our sea-washed, sunset gates shall stand
A mighty woman with a torch, whose flame
Is the imprisoned lightning, and her name
Mother of Exiles. From her beacon-hand
Glows world-wide welcome; her mild eyes command
The air-bridged harbor that twin cities frame.
"Keep, ancient lands, your storied pomp!" cries she
With silent lips. "Give me your tired, your poor,
Your huddled masses yearning to breathe free,
The wretched refuse of your teeming shore.
Send these, the homeless, tempest-tost to me,
I lift my lamp beside the golden door!"

(Written in 1883. The Statue of Liberty was unveiled in 1886.)

# OPPORTUNITY

John James Ingalls

Master of human destinics am I!
Fame, love, and fortune on my footsteps wait.
Cities and fields I walk; I penetrate
Deserts and seas remote, and passing by
Hovel and mart and palace—soon or late
I knock unbidden once at every gate!

If sleeping, wake—if feasting, rise before
I turn away. It is the hour of fate,
And they who follow me reach every state
Mortals desire, and conquer every foe
Save death; but those who doubt or hesitate,
Condemned to failure, penury and woe,
Seek me in vain and uselessly implore.
I answer not, and I return no more!

# THE WHEEL THAT SQUEAKS

Henry Wheeler Shaw ("Josh Billings")

The wheel that squeaks the loudest
Is the one that gets the grease.

—From "The Kicker"

## MY SYMPHONY
### William Henry Channing

To live content with small means; to seek elegance rather than luxury, and refinement rather than fashion; to be worthy, not respectable, and wealthy, not rich; to study hard, think quietly, talk gently, act frankly; to listen to stars and birds, to babes and sages, with open heart; to bear all cheerfully, do all bravely, await occasions, hurry never. In a word, to let the spiritual, unbidden and unconscious, grow up through the common. This is my symphony.

## AN OPEN WOOD-FIRE
### Thomas Bailey Aldrich

What is more cheerful, now, in the fall of the year, than an open wood-fire? Do you hear those little chirps and twitters coming out of that piece of apple-wood? Those are the ghosts of the robins and bluebirds that sang upon the bough when it was in blossom last spring. In summer whole flocks of them come fluttering about the fruit-trees under the window: so I have singing birds all the year round.

—From "Miss Mehitabel's Son"

## ADVICE TO WRITERS
## FOR THE DAILY PRESS

### Joel Chandler Harris

When you've got a thing to say,
Say it! Don't take half a day.
When your tale's got little in it,
Crowd the whole thing in a minute!
Life is short—a fleeting vapor—
Don't you fill the whole blamed paper
With a tale which, at a pinch,
Could be cornered in an inch!
Boil her down until she simmers,
Polish her until she glimmers.

## LIVING

### Anonymous

To touch the cup with eager lips and taste, not drain it;
To woo and tempt and court a bliss—and not attain it;
To fondle and caress a joy, yet hold it lightly,
Lest it become necessity and cling too tightly;
To watch the sun set in the west without regretting;
To hail its advent in the east—the night forgetting;
To smother care in happiness and grief in laughter;
To hold the present close—not questioning hereafter;
To have enough to share—to know the joy of giving;
To thrill with all the sweets of life—is living.

[ 267 ]

## PUDD'NHEAD WILSON'S CALENDAR

### Mark Twain (Samuel L. Clemens)

Training is everything. The peach was once a bitter almond; cauliflower is nothing but cabbage with a college education.

\* \* \*

One of the most striking differences between a cat and a lie is that a cat has only nine lives.

\* \* \*

Consider well the proportions of things. It is better to be a young June-bug than an old bird of paradise.

\* \* \*

It is easy to find fault, if one has that disposition. There was once a man who, not being able to find any other fault with his coal, complained that there were too many prehistoric toads in it.

—From *Pudd'nhead Wilson*

## THE PESSIMIST
### Ben King

Nothing to do but work,
  Nothing to eat but food,
Nothing to wear but clothes
  To keep one from going nude.

Nothing to breathe but air,
  Quick as a flash 'tis gone;
Nowhere to fall but off,
  Nowhere to stand but on.

Nothing to comb but hair,
  Nowhere to sleep but in bed;
Nothing to weep but tears,
  Nothing to bury but dead.

Nothing to sing but songs,
  Ah, well, alas! alack!
Nowhere to go but out,
  Nowhere to come but back.

Nothing to see but sights,
  Nothing to quench but thirst,
Nothing to have but what we've got;
  Thus thro' life we are cursed.

Nothing to strike but a gait;
  Everything moves that goes.
Nothing at all but common sense
  Can ever withstand these woes.

# THE HOUSE BY
# THE SIDE OF THE ROAD

Sam Walter Foss

There are hermit souls that live withdrawn
  In the peace of their self-content;
There are souls, like stars, that dwell apart
  In a fellowless firmament;
There are pioneer souls that blaze their paths
  Where highways never ran;—
But let me live by the side of the road
  And be a friend to man.

Let me live in a house by the side of the road,
  Where the race of men go by—
The men who are good and the men who are bad,
  As good and as bad as I.
I would not sit in the scorner's seat,
  Or hurl the cynic's ban;—
Let me live in a house by the side of the road
  And be a friend to man.

I see from my house by the side of the road,
  By the side of the highway of life,
The men who press with the ardor of hope,
  The men who are faint with the strife.
But I turn not away from their smiles nor their tears,
  Both parts of an infinite plan;—
Let me live in my house by the side of the road
  And be a friend to man.

I know there are brook-gladdened meadows ahead
  And mountains of wearisome height;

That the road passes on through the long afternoon
  And stretches away to the night.
But still I rejoice when the travelers rejoice,
  And weep with the strangers that moan,
Nor live in my house by the side of the road
  Like a man who dwells alone.

Let me live in my house by the side of the road
  Where the race of men go by;—
They are good, they are bad, they are weak, they are strong,
  Wise, foolish—so am I.
Then why should I sit in the scorner's seat,
  Or hurl the cynic's ban?—
Let me live in my house by the side of the road
  And be a friend to man.

## FOUR THINGS

Henry van Dyke

Four things a man must learn to do
If he would make his record true:
To think without confusion clearly;
To love his fellow men sincerely;
To act from honest motives purely;
To trust in God and Heaven securely.

## LIFE, A QUESTION

Corinne Roosevelt Robinson

Life? and worth living?
Yes, with each part of us—
Hurt of us, help of us,
      hope of us, heart of us,
Life is worth living.
Ah! with the whole of us,
Will of us, brain of us,
      senses and soul of us.
Is life worth living?
Aye, with the best of us,
Heights of us, depths of us—
Life is the test of us!

## DO YOU FEAR THE WIND?

Hamlin Garland

Do you fear the force of the wind,
The slash of the rain?
Go face them and fight them,
Be savage again.
Go hungry and cold like the wolf,
  Go wade like the crane;
The palms of your hands will thicken,
The skin of your cheek will tan,
You'll grow ragged and weary and swarthy,
  But you'll walk like a man!

## TO THE BOYS OF AMERICA

Theodore Roosevelt

Of course what we have a right to expect from the American boy is that he shall turn out to be a good American man. Now, the chances are strong that he won't be much of a man unless he is a good deal of a boy. He must not be a coward or a weakling, a bully, a shirk or a prig. He must work hard and play hard. He must be clean-minded and clean-lived, and able to hold his own under all circumstances and against all comers. It is only on these conditions that he will grow into the kind of man of whom America can really be proud. . . . In short, in life, as in a football game, the principle to follow is: Hit the line hard; don't foul and don't shirk, but hit the line hard.

—From "The American Boy"

## THE FLAG GOES BY

### Henry Holcomb Bennett

Hats off!
Along the street there comes
A blare of bugles, a ruffle of drums,
A flash of color beneath the sky:
Hats off!
The flag is passing by!

Blue and crimson and white it shines,
Over the steel-tipped, ordered lines.
Hats off!
The colors before us fly;
But more than the flag is passing by:
Sea-fights and land-fights, grim and great,
Fought to make and to save the State;
Weary marches and sinking ships;
Cheers of victory on dying lips;

Days of plenty and years of peace;
March of a strong land's swift increase;
Equal justice, right and law,
Stately honor and reverend awe;

Sign of a nation great and strong
To ward her people from foreign wrong;
Pride and glory and honor—all
Live in the colors to stand or fall.

Hats off!
Along the street there comes
A blare of bugles, a ruffle of drums;
And loyal hearts are beating high:
Hats off!
The flag is passing by!

## WE STAND AT ARMAGEDDON

### Theodore Roosevelt

We fight in honorable fashion for the good of mankind; fearless of the future, unheeding of our individual fates, with unflinching hearts and undimmed eyes; we stand at Armageddon, and we battle for the Lord.

—From a speech at Chicago, June 17, 1912

## THEODORE ROOSEVELT SAID

I wish to preach, not the doctrine of ignoble
ease, but the doctrine of the strenuous life.

\* \* \*

There is a homely old adage which runs, "Speak softly and carry a big stick; you will go far." If the American nation will speak softly and yet build and keep at a pitch of the highest training a thoroughly efficient navy, the Monroe Doctrine will go far.

\* \* \*

When you play, play hard, but
when you work, don't play at all.

[ 275 ]

## WOODROW WILSON SAID

The world must be made safe for democracy.

## CONGRESS IS ASKED TO DECLARE WAR
### Woodrow Wilson

... It is a fearful thing to lead this great peaceful people into war, into the most terrible and disastrous of all wars, civilization itself seeming to be in the balance. But the right is more precious than peace, and we shall fight for the things which we have always carried nearest our hearts—for democracy, for the right of those who submit to authority to have a voice in their own governments, for the rights and liberties of small nations, for a universal dominion of right by such a concert of free peoples as shall bring peace and safety to all nations and make the world itself at last free.

To such a task we can dedicate our lives and our fortunes, everything that we are and everything that we have, with the pride of those who know that the day has come when America is privileged to spend her blood and her might for the principles that gave her birth and happiness and the peace which she has treasured. God helping her, she can do no other.

—From *Address to Congress,* April 2, 1917

# THE MARINES' SONG

Anonymous

From the Halls of Montezuma
To the shores of Tripoli
We fight our country's battles
On the land as on the sea.
First to fight for right and freedom
And to keep our honor clean;
We are proud to claim the title
Of United States Marines.

Our flag's unfurled to every breeze
From dawn to setting sun;
We have fought in every clime and place
Where we could take a gun.
In the snow of far-off Northern lands
And in sunny tropic scenes;
You will find us always on the job—
The United States Marines.

Here's health to you and to our Corps
Which we are proud to serve;
In many a strife we've fought for life
And never lost our nerve.
If the Army and the Navy
Ever look on Heaven's scenes,
They will find the streets are guarded
By United States Marines.

## THE CAISSON SONG

Major Edmund L. Gruber

Over hill, over dale, we have hit the dusty trail,
And those caissons go rolling along.
In and out, hear them shout, "Counter march and right about!"
And those caissons go rolling along.

*Chorus:*

Then it's hi! hi! hee! in the field artillery,
Sound off your numbers loud and strong.
Where e'er you go you will always know
That those caissons are rolling along.
Keep them rolling! And those caissons go rolling along.
Then it's Battery Halt!

Through the storm, through the night, up to where the
doughboys fight,
All our caissons go rolling along.
At zero we'll be there, answering every call and flare,
While our caissons go rolling along.

Cavalry, boot to boot, we will join in the pursuit,
While the caissons go rolling along.

Action front, at a trot; volley fire with shell and shot,
While those caissons go rolling along.

But if fate me should call, and in action I should fall,
And those caissons go rolling along,
Fire at will, lay 'em low, never stop for any foe,
While those caissons go rolling along.

But if fate me should call, and in action I should fall,
Keep those caissons a-rolling along.
Then in peace I'll abide when I take my final ride
On a caisson that's rolling along.

## OUR COUNTRY

Anna Louise Dabney

Our country is a tapestry,
  Woven by loving hands;
By Faith and Hope 'twas deftly made
  From threads of other lands;
And each retains its native hue
  Whose beauty animates
A varied pattern, lovely, new—
  Our own United States.

## WORDS FOR ARMY BUGLE CALLS

Anonymous

### REVEILLE

I can't get 'em up, I can't get 'em up,
I can't get 'em up in the morning.
I can't get 'em up, I can't get 'em up,
I can't get 'em up at all.
The corp'ral's worse than privates;
The sergeant's worse than corp'rals;
Lieutenant's worse than sergeants;
An' the captain's worst of all!

### SICK CALL

Come and get your quinine,
    And come and get your pills;
Oh! Come and get your quinine,
And cure, and cure,
    All your ills, and cure your ills.

### MESS CALL

Soupy, soupy, soupy,
    Without a single bean;
Porky, porky, porky,
    Without a streak of lean;
Coffee, coffee, coffee,
    Without any cream.

### STABLE CALL

Come off to the stable, all you who are able,
And give your horses some oats and some corn;
For if you don't do it, your colonel will know it,
And then you will rue it, as sure as you're born.

### FATIGUE CALL

With a pick and with a shovel, and with a hoe;
With a sentry at your back you won't say no;
With a pick and with a shovel, and with a hoe,
Down in the ditch you go!

### TAPS

Fading light
Dims the sight,
And a star gems the sky,
Gleaming bright;
From a-far,
Drawing nigh,
Falls the night.

## THE AMERICAN CREED

William Tyler Page

*I believe in the United States of America* as a government of the people, by the people, for the people; whose just powers are derived from the consent of the governed; a democracy in a republic; a sovereign nation of many sovereign states; a perfect union, one and inseparable; established upon those principles of freedom, equality, justice, and humanity for which American patriots sacrificed their lives and fortunes.

*I therefore believe it is my duty to my country* to love it; to support its Constitution; to obey its laws; to respect its flag, and to defend it against all enemies.

—(Accepted, April 3, 1918, by the House of Representatives on behalf of the American People)

## INSCRIPTION ON THE TOMB OF
## THE UNKNOWN SOLDIER

Here Rests in
Honored Glory
An American
Soldier
Known But to God

## CONDENSED HISTORY LESSON

Asked if he could summarize the lessons of history in a short book, Charles A. Beard said he could do it in four sentences.

(1) Whom the gods would destroy, they first make mad with power.
(2) The mills of God grind slowly, but they grind exceeding small.
(3) The bee fertilizes the flower it robs.
(4) When it is dark enough, you can see the stars.

—Contributed by Arthur H. Secord to *The Readers Digest*

# I BELIEVE

## John D. Rockefeller, Jr.

I believe in the supreme worth of the individual and in his right to life, liberty, and the pursuit of happiness.

I believe that every right implies a responsibility; every opportunity, an obligation; every possession, a duty.

I believe that the law was made for man and not man for the law; that government is the servant of the people and not their master.

I believe in the dignity of labor, whether with head or hand; that the world owes no man a living but that it owes every man an opportunity to make a living.

I believe that thrift is essential to well-ordered living and that economy is prime requisite of a sound financial structure, whether in government, business, or personal affairs.

I believe that truth and justice are fundamental to an enduring social order.

I believe in the sacredness of a promise, that a man's word should be as good as his bond; that character—not wealth or power or position—is of supreme worth.

I believe that the rendering of useful service is the common duty of mankind and that only in the purifying fire of sacrifice is the dross of selfishness consumed and the greatness of the human soul set free.

I believe in an all-wise and all-loving God, named by whatever name, and that the individual's highest fulfillment, greatest happiness, and widest usefulness are to be found in living in harmony with His will.

I believe that love is the greatest thing in the world; that right can and will triumph over might.

## THE FOUR FREEDOMS
Franklin Delano Roosevelt

In the future days which we seek to make secure, we look forward to a world founded upon four essential freedoms.

The first is freedom of speech and expression—everywhere in the world.

The second is freedom of every person to worship God in his own way—everywhere in the world.

The third is freedom from want, which, translated into world terms, means economic understanding which will secure to every nation a healthy peacetime life for its inhabitants—everywhere in the world.

The fourth is freedom from fear, which, translated into world terms, means a world-wide reduction of armaments to such a point and in such a thorough fashion that no nation will be in a position to commit an act of physical aggression against any neighbor—anywhere in the world.

—From an address to Congress, January 6, 1941

## AMERICA THE BEAUTIFUL

Katharine Lee Bates

O beautiful for spacious skies,
For amber waves of grain,
For purple mountain majesties
Above the fruited plain!
America! America!
God shed His grace on thee
And crown thy good with brotherhood
From sea to shining sea!

O beautiful for pilgrim feet,
Whose stern, impassioned stress
A thoroughfare for freedom beat
Across the wilderness!
America! America!
God mend thine every flaw,
Confirm thy soul in self-control,
Thy liberty in law!

O beautiful for heroes proved
In liberating strife,

Who more than self their country loved,
And mercy more than life!
America! America!
May God thy gold refine
Till all success be nobleness
And every gain divine!

O beautiful for patriot dream
That sees beyond the years
Thine alabaster cities gleam
Undimmed by human tears!
America! America!
God shed His grace on thee
And crown thy good with brotherhood
From sea to shining sea!

# INDEX OF AUTHORS,
## TITLES AND FIRST LINES

# INDEX OF AUTHORS, TITLES AND FIRST LINES

*Names of authors appear in capital letters;
titles in roman; and first lines in italics.*

PAGE

ABBEY, HENRY (1842-1911)
What Do We Plant? . . . . . . . . . 143
*A boy and his dog make a glorious pair* . . . . . . . 25
ADAMS, SAMUEL (1722-1803)
On Freedom of Thought . . . . . . . . 182
*A dreary place would be this earth* . . . . . . . . 49
Adventure . . . . . . . . . . . 19
Advice to Writers for the Daily Press . . . . . . . 267
*A fly and a flea in a flue* . . . . . . . . . . 110
*After four years of arduous service* . . . . . . . . 240
*A house divided against itself* . . . . . . . . . 225
Aladdin . . . . . . . . . . . 85
ALDIS, DOROTHY
It Was . . . . . . . . . . . 20
My Nose . . . . . . . . . . . 23
ALDRICH, THOMAS BAILEY (1836-1907)
An Open Wood-Fire . . . . . . . . . 266
Miss Mehitabel's Son (*selection from*) . . . . . . 266
*A little word in kindness spoken* . . . . . . . . 112
ALLEN, ELIZABETH AKERS (1832-1911)
Rock Me to Sleep . . . . . . . . . 125
Almanac for Moderns, An (*selection from*) . . . . . . 85
*A man is rich in proportion* . . . . . . . . . 209
Ambitious Mouse, The . . . . . . . . . 19
America . . . . . . . . . . . 190
America for Me . . . . . . . . . . 261
*America is God's Crucible* . . . . . . . . . 252
American Boy, The (*selection from*) . . . . . . . 273
American Creed, The . . . . . . . . . 282
American Flag, The . . . . . . . . . 187
America the Beautiful . . . . . . . . . 286
*And what is so rare as a day in June* . . . . . . . 106

[ 291 ]

Animal Crackers . . . . . . . . . . . . . . . 23
*Announced by all the trumpets of the sky* . . . . . . 140
ANONYMOUS
    Adventure . . . . . . . . . . . . . . 19
    Beautiful . . . . . . . . . . . . . . . 38
    Boston . . . . . . . . . . . . . . . 251
    Bury Me Not on the Lone Prairie . . . . . . . 256
    Green Grass Growing All Around, The . . . . . . 81
    Home on the Range . . . . . . . . . . . 254
    How to Tell Bad News . . . . . . . . . 102
    I've Been Workin' on the Railroad . . . . . . 253
    Lend a Hand . . . . . . . . . . . . 122
    Limericks . . . . . . . . . . . . . 110
    Little Willie . . . . . . . . . . . . 73
    Living . . . . . . . . . . . . . . 267
    Marines' Song, The . . . . . . . . . . . 277
    Merry Sunshine . . . . . . . . . . . . 66
    Nonsense Jingles . . . . . . . . . . . 92
    Our Lips and Ears . . . . . . . . . . . 128
    Persevere . . . . . . . . . . . . . 38
    Salute to Our Flag . . . . . . . . . . . 148
    Sunset . . . . . . . . . . . . . . 77
    Ten Little Injuns . . . . . . . . . . . 80
    There Was a Little Girl . . . . . . . . . 31
    We Thank Thee . . . . . . . . . . . 28
    Words for Army Bugle Calls . . . . . . . 280
    Work While You Work . . . . . . . . . 58
    Yankee Doodle . . . . . . . . . . . 170
April Rain . . . . . . . . . . . . . . . 86
Are We a Nation? *(selection from)* . . . . . . . 247
*A road might lead to anywhere* . . . . . . . . . 144
Arrow and the Song, The . . . . . . . . . . 108
Arsenal at Springfield, The *(selection from)* . . . . . 222
Art *(selections from)* . . . . . . . . . . . 213
*As a beauty I am not a star* . . . . . . . . . 110
*As I would not be a slave* . . . . . . . . . . 225
*A slip of the foot* . . . . . . . . . . . . 169
Autumn . . . . . . . . . . . . . . . 87
*A wise old owl sat on an oak* . . . . . . . . . 61
Axis of the Earth, The . . . . . . . . . . 217
*Ay, tear her tattered ensign down* . . . . . . . 197

[ 292 ]

Baby-Land . . . . . . . . . . . . . . . 51
*Backward, turn backward, O Time* . . . . . . . . 125
Baker's Duzzen uv Wize Sawz, A . . . . . . . . . 90
BANGS, JOHN KENDRICK (1862-1922)
    Little Elf-Man, The . . . . . . . . . 24
Barbara Frietchie . . . . . . . . . . . . . 232
Barefoot Boy, The . . . . . . . . . . . . . 29
Barter . . . . . . . . . . . . . . . . 91
BATES, DAVID (1810-1876)
    Speak Gently . . . . . . . . . . 129
BATES, KATHERINE LEE (1859-1929)
    America the Beautiful . . . . . . . . . 286
Battle-Field, The *(selection from)* . . . . . . . 241
Battle-Hymn of the Republic . . . . . . . . . . 230
BEARD, CHARLES A. (1874-1948)
    Condensed History Lesson . . . . . . . . 283
Beautiful . . . . . . . . . . . . . . 38
*Beautiful faces are they that wear* . . . . . . . 38
Be Courteous to All . . . . . . . . . . . . 171
*Before her supper where she sits* . . . . . . . 21
Behavior *(selection from)* . . . . . . . . . . 141
*Behind him lay the gray Azores* . . . . . . . . 153
Bells, The . . . . . . . . . . . . . . . 99
BENÉT, ROSEMARY
    Nancy Hanks . . . . . . . . . . . . . 226
BENNETT, HENRY HOLCOMB (1863-1924)
    Flag Goes By, The . . . . . . . . . . 274
Be Noble! . . . . . . . . . . . . . . 217
*Between the dark and the daylight* . . . . . . . 26
Bible, The . . . . . . . . . . . . . . 216
BILLINGS, JOSH (see Henry Wheeler Shaw)
Bird Music . . . . . . . . . . . . . . 85
*Blessings on thee, little man* . . . . . . . . . 29
Blue and the Gray, The . . . . . . . . . . . 245
Book, A. . . . . . . . . . . . . . . . 87
Boston . . . . . . . . . . . . . . . . 251
Boy and His Dog, A . . . . . . . . . . . . 25
Boy Scout Oath, The . . . . . . . . . . . 149
BRALEY, BERTON (1882-    )
    Opportunity . . . . . . . . . . . . . 130

BREWER, EBENEZER COBHAM (1810 -1897)
    Little Things . . . . . . . . . . . . . . . . . 32
Brown Thrush, The . . . . . . . . . . . . . . . . 22
BRYANT, WILLIAM CULLEN (1794-1878)
    Battle-Field, The (*selection from*) . . . . . . . . 241
    Death of the Flowers (*selection from*) . . . . . . 105
    Melancholy Days, The . . . . . . . . . . . . 105
    O Mother of a Mighty Race . . . . . . . . . 206
    Robert of Lincoln . . . . . . . . . . . . . 70
    Song of Marion's Men . . . . . . . . . . . . 185
    Thanatopsis (*selection from*) . . . . . . . . 136
    Truth, the Invincible . . . . . . . . . . . 241
Building of the Ship, The (*selection from*) . . . . . . 219
BURGESS, FRANK GELETT (1866-    )
    On Digital Extremities . . . . . . . . . . . . 120
    Purple Cow, The . . . . . . . . . . . . . 61
Bury Me Not on the Lone Prairie . . . . . . . . . 256
By Blue Ontario's Shore (*selection from*) . . . . . . . 251
Byron (*selection from*) . . . . . . . . . . . . 251
By the flow of the inland river . . . . . . . . . 245
By the rude bridge that arched the flood . . . . . . . 179
By the shores of Gitchee Gumee . . . . . . . . . 155


Caisson Song, The . . . . . . . . . . . . . . 278
Casey at the Bat . . . . . . . . . . . . . . . 88
CHANNING, WILLIAM HENRY (1810-1884)
    My Symphony . . . . . . . . . . . . . . 266
Chapel of the Hermit, The (*selection from*) . . . . . . 250
CHAPMAN, ARTHUR (1873-1935)
    Out Where the West Begins . . . . . . . . . 255
Charles Sumner (*selection from*) . . . . . . . . . 253
CHASE, SALMON PORTLAND (1808-1873)
    Constitution, The . . . . . . . . . . . . . 215
CHILD, LYDIA MARIA (1802-1880)
    Thanksgiving Day . . . . . . . . . . . . . 62
Children's Hour, The . . . . . . . . . . . . . 26
Christmas Bells . . . . . . . . . . . . . . . 228
CHURCH, FRANCIS PHARCELLUS (1839-1906)
    Is There a Santa Claus? . . . . . . . . . . . 42
Circles (*selection from*) . . . . . . . . . . . . 213

Civilization (*selection from*) . . . . . . . . . . . . . . 213
CLAY, HENRY (1777-1852)
    I Would Rather Be Right . . . . . . . . . . . . 200
CLEMENS, SAMUEL L. (see Mark Twain)
COATSWORTH, ELIZABETH J. (1893-    )
    Counters . . . . . . . . . . . . . . . . . . . 133
    Wilderness Is Tamed, The . . . . . . . . . . 205
COLESWORTHY, DANIEL CLEMENT (1810-1893)
    Little Word, A . . . . . . . . . . . . . . . . 112
Columbus . . . . . . . . . . . . . . . . . . . . . 153
*Come and get your quinine* . . . . . . . . . . . . 280
*"Come, little leaves," said the wind* . . . . . . . . . 65
*Come off to the stable* . . . . . . . . . . . . . . 281
Concord Hymn, The . . . . . . . . . . . . . . . 179
Condensed History Lesson . . . . . . . . . . . . 283
Congress Is Asked to Declare War . . . . . . . . 276
*Consider well the proportions* . . . . . . . . . . . 268
Constitution, Preamble to the . . . . . . . . . . 187
Constitution, The . . . . . . . . . . . . . . . . 215
COOKE, EDMUND VANCE (1866-1932)
    Well, Did You Hear? . . . . . . . . . . . . . 196
COOPER, GEORGE (1840-1927)
    Baby-Land . . . . . . . . . . . . . . . . . . 51
    Wind and the Leaves, The . . . . . . . . . . 65
Counters . . . . . . . . . . . . . . . . . . . . . 133
CROCKETT, DAVID (1786-1836)
    Motto . . . . . . . . . . . . . . . . . . . . 203


DABNEY, ANNA LOUISE
    Our Country . . . . . . . . . . . . . . . . . 279
*Dashing thro' the snow* . . . . . . . . . . . . . 109
Daughter at Evening, The . . . . . . . . . . . . 21
David Crockett's Motto . . . . . . . . . . . . . 203
David Harum (*selection from*) . . . . . . . . . . 101
Day Is Done, The . . . . . . . . . . . . . . . . 96
Day's Demand, The . . . . . . . . . . . . . . . 220
*Dear common flower, that grow'st* . . . . . . . . . 37
*Dear Madam: I have been shown* . . . . . . . . . 239
*Dear mother, how pretty* . . . . . . . . . . . . 60
Death of the Flowers, The (*selection from*) . . . . . . 105

Declaration of Independence, The (*selection from*) . . . . 181
Democracy (*selection from*) . . . . . . . . . . . 204
DICKINSON, EMILY (1830-1886)
    Autumn . . . . . . . . . . . . . . . 87
    Book, A . . . . . . . . . . . . . . . 87
    Pedigree . . . . . . . . . . . . . . 137
    Poetry . . . . . . . . . . . . . . . 259
    Railway Train, The . . . . . . . . . . . 73
    There Is No Frigate Like a Book . . . . . . 145
Difference, The . . . . . . . . . . . . . . . 24
Dinkey-Bird, The . . . . . . . . . . . . . . 30
Dixie . . . . . . . . . . . . . . . . . . 227
*Don't throw stones at your neighbors* . . . . . . . . 169
*Dost thou love life?* . . . . . . . . . . . . . 169
DOUGLAS, MARIAN
    Pert Chicken, The . . . . . . . . . . . 119
Do You Fear the Wind? . . . . . . . . . . . . 272
DRAKE, JOSEPH RODMAN (1795-1820)
    American Flag, The . . . . . . . . . . . 187
Duel, The . . . . . . . . . . . . . . . . 34
Duty . . . . . . . . . . . . . . . . . 86

*Early to bed and early to rise* . . . . . . . . . . 169
*Eight fingers, Ten toes* . . . . . . . . . . . . 24
Elf and the Dormouse, The . . . . . . . . . . 50
Elizabeth (*selection from*) . . . . . . . . . . . 136
EMERSON, RALPH WALDO (1803-1882)
    Art (*selections from*) . . . . . . . . . . 213
    Behavior (*selection from*) . . . . . . . . 141
    Circles (*selection from*) . . . . . . . . . 213
    Civilization (*selection from*) . . . . . . . . 213
    Concord Hymn, The . . . . . . . . . . . 179
    Duty . . . . . . . . . . . . . . . . 86
    Enthusiasm . . . . . . . . . . . . . . 213
    Every Genuine Work of Art . . . . . . . . 213
    Forbearance . . . . . . . . . . . . . 103
    Mountain and the Squirrel, The . . . . . . . 56
    Nation's Strength, A . . . . . . . . . . 218
    Or Make a Better Mousetrap . . . . . . . . 216
    Snow Storm, The . . . . . . . . . . . 140
    There Is Always a Best Way . . . . . . . . 141

EMERSON, (*Continued*)

    To Find the Beautiful . . . . . . . . . . . . . 213

    Voluntaries (*selection from*) . . . . . . . . . . 86

    We Thank Thee . . . . . . . . . . . . . 28

    Wisdom of a Man, The . . . . . . . . . . . 213

EMMETT, DANIEL DECATUR (1815-1904)

    Dixie . . . . . . . . . . . . . . . . 227

Enthusiasm . . . . . . . . . . . . . . . . 213

En Voyage . . . . . . . . . . . . . . . . 94

Eternal Partnership . . . . . . . . . . . . . 95

Eternal Struggle, The . . . . . . . . . . . . 223

*Eternal vigilance is the price* . . . . . . . . . . 218

Eulogy of the Dog . . . . . . . . . . . . . 100

EUWER, ANTHONY HENDERSON (1877-    )

    My Face (limerick) . . . . . . . . . . . . 110

Evangeline (*selections from*) . . . . . . . . . 123, 132

EVERETT, DAVID (1769-1813)

    Tall Oaks from Little Acorns . . . . . . . . 55

Every Genuine Work of Art . . . . . . . . . . 213


*Fading light Dims the sight* . . . . . . . . . . . 281

FARRAR, JOHN (1896-    )

    Ambitious Mouse, The . . . . . . . . . . 19

*Father and I went down to camp* . . . . . . . . 170

*Father calls me William* . . . . . . . . . . . 44

Father's Education . . . . . . . . . . . . . 101

Fatigue Call . . . . . . . . . . . . . . . 281

Fer a Dog . . . . . . . . . . . . . . . 101

FIELD, EUGENE (1850-1895)

    Dinkey-Bird, The . . . . . . . . . . . . 30

    Duel, The . . . . . . . . . . . . . . 34

    Jest 'fore Christmas . . . . . . . . . . . 44

    Little Boy Blue . . . . . . . . . . . . . 41

    Rock-A-Bye Lady, The . . . . . . . . . . 48

    Seein' Things . . . . . . . . . . . . . 64

    Sugar-Plum Tree, The . . . . . . . . . . . 67

    Wynken, Blynken, and Nod . . . . . . . . . 74

FIELD, RACHEL (1894-1942)

    For Christmas . . . . . . . . . . . . . 95

    Roads . . . . . . . . . . . . . . . 144

FINCH, FRANCIS MILES (1827-1907)
    Blue and the Gray, The . . . . . . . . . . . . 245
    Nathan Hale . . . . . . . . . . . . . . . 183
First in War, First in Peace . . . . . . . . . . . 191
First "Morgan," The . . . . . . . . . . . . . . 198
First Snow-Fall, The . . . . . . . . . . . . . . 98
Flag Goes By, The . . . . . . . . . . . . . . . 274
Fog . . . . . . . . . . . . . . . . . . . . 98
FOLLEN, ELIZA LEE (1787-1860)
    New Moon, The . . . . . . . . . . . . . . 60
    Three Little Kittens, The . . . . . . . . . . 68
Forbearance . . . . . . . . . . . . . . . . . 103
For Christmas . . . . . . . . . . . . . . . . 95
Forest Primeval, The . . . . . . . . . . . . . 123
*For mother-love and father-care* . . . . . . . . . 28
For of All Sad Words . . . . . . . . . . . . . 93
*"For this true nobleness I seek* . . . . . . . . . . 217
*For want of a nail* . . . . . . . . . . . . . . 169
FOSS, SAM WALTER (1858-1911)
    House by the Side of the Road, The . . . . . . . 270
FOSTER, STEPHEN COLLINS (1825-1864)
    My Old Kentucky Home . . . . . . . . . . . 211
    Old Folks at Home . . . . . . . . . . . . 210
Four Freedoms, The . . . . . . . . . . . . . . 285
Four-Leaf Clover . . . . . . . . . . . . . . . 35
*Fourscore and seven years ago* . . . . . . . . . . 238
Four Things . . . . . . . . . . . . . . . . 271
*Four things a man must learn to do* . . . . . . . . 271
Fourth of July Ode . . . . . . . . . . . . . . 192
FRANKLIN, BENJAMIN (1706-1790)
    Here Is My Creed . . . . . . . . . . . . . 167
    Rapid Progress of True Science, The . . . . . . 186
    Sayings of "Poor Richard" . . . . . . . . . . 168
*Freedom of thought and the right* . . . . . . . . 182
*From the Halls of Montezuma* . . . . . . . . . . 277
FROST, ROBERT (1875-    )
    Pasture, The . . . . . . . . . . . . . . . 123
    Runaway, The . . . . . . . . . . . . . . 76

GARLAND, HAMLIN (1860-1940)
    Do You Fear the Wind? . . . . . . . . . . . 272

*Gentlemen of the Jury: The best friend* . . . . . . . . . . 100
George Washington and the Cherry Tree . . . . . . . . . 166
Gettysburg Address, The . . . . . . . . . . . . . 238
GIBBONS, JAMES SLOANE (1810-1892)
    Three Hundred Thousand More . . . . . . . . 231
GILMORE, PATRICK S. (1829-1892)
    When Johnny Comes Marching Home . . . . . 243
Girl Scout Promise, The . . . . . . . . . . . . . 149
Give Me Liberty or Give Me Death! . . . . . . . . 172
*"Give me of your bark, O Birch-tree!* . . . . . . . . 158
Glance Behind the Curtain, A *(selection from)* . . . . . 260
Go Confidently! . . . . . . . . . . . . . . . 209
*God give us men! A time like this demands* . . . . . . 220
God Grants Liberty . . . . . . . . . . . . . . 203
*God helps them* . . . . . . . . . . . . . . . 169
*"Good-morning, Merry Sunshine"* . . . . . . . . . 66
Good Night . . . . . . . . . . . . . . . . 27
GOODRICH, SAMUEL GRISWOLD (Peter Parley) (1793-1860)
    Good Night . . . . . . . . . . . . . . 27
Go West, Young Man . . . . . . . . . . . . . 254
Gradatim *(selection from)* . . . . . . . . . . . . 112
*Great beauty, great strength* . . . . . . . . . . . 168
Great Melting Pot, The . . . . . . . . . . . . 252
GREELEY, HORACE (1811-1872)
    Go West, Young Man . . . . . . . . . . . 254
Green Grass Growing All Around, The . . . . . . . . 81
GRUBER, MAJOR EDMUND L. (1879-   )
    Caisson Song, The . . . . . . . . . . . . 278
GUEST, EDGAR A. (1881-   )
    Boy and His Dog, A . . . . . . . . . . . . 25
    Home . . . . . . . . . . . . . . . . 121
    It Couldn't Be Done . . . . . . . . . . . 135

Hail, Columbia . . . . . . . . . . . . . . . 194
HALE, EDWARD EVERETT (1822-1909)
    Look Up . . . . . . . . . . . . . . . 115
    Your Country . . . . . . . . . . . . . 196
HALE, NATHAN (1755-1776)
    His Last Words . . . . . . . . . . . . . 186
HALE, SARAH JOSEPHA (1788-1879)
    Mary's Lamb . . . . . . . . . . . . . . 59

Hands of Toil, The . . . . . . . . . . . . . 260
HARRIS, JOEL CHANDLER (1848-1908)
    Advice to Writers for the Daily Press . . . . . . 267
*Ha! Steward, how are you* . . . . . . . . . . . 102
*Hast thou named all the birds* . . . . . . . . . 103
*Hats off! Along the street* . . . . . . . . . . . 274
*Have you ever heard of the Sugar-Plum Tree?* . . . . . 67
*Hear the sledges with the bells* . . . . . . . . . 99
*He ate and drank the precious words* . . . . . . . . 87
*Heaven is not reached at a single bound* . . . . . . . 112
Height of the Ridiculous, The . . . . . . . . . 104
*He killed the noble Mudjokivis* . . . . . . . . . . 91
HEMANS, FELICIA DOROTHEA (1793-1835)
    Landing of the Pilgrim Fathers . . . . . . . 163
Henry Clay Said . . . . . . . . . . . . . . 200
HENRY, MARGUERITE
    First "Morgan," The . . . . . . . . . . 198
HENRY, PATRICK (1736-1799)
    Give Me Liberty or Give Me Death . . . . . . 172
Hens, The . . . . . . . . . . . . . . . . 33
*He or she is greatest who contributes* . . . . . . . . 251
Here Is My Creed . . . . . . . . . . . . . 167
*Here Rests in Honored Glory* . . . . . . . . . . 283
*Here's an adventure! what awaits* . . . . . . . . . 19
HERFORD, OLIVER (1863-1935)
    Elf and the Dormouse, The . . . . . . . . 50
*He that scatters thorns* . . . . . . . . . . . . 169
*He that would live in peace* . . . . . . . . . . . 168
Hiawatha's Childhood . . . . . . . . . . . . 155
Hiawatha's Sailing . . . . . . . . . . . . . 158
*Hide not your talents* . . . . . . . . . . . . 168
HIGGINSON, ELLA (1862-1940)
    Four-Leaf Clover . . . . . . . . . . . . 35
HOLLAND, JOSIAH GILBERT (1819-1881)
    Day's Demand, The . . . . . . . . . . . 220
    Gradatim (*selection from*) . . . . . . . . 112
    Ladder, The . . . . . . . . . . . . . 112
    Wanted (*selection from*) . . . . . . . . . 220
HOLMES, OLIVER WENDELL (1809-1894)
    Autocrat of the Breakfast Table, The (*selection from*) 217
    Axis of the Earth, The . . . . . . . . . . 217

HOLMES, (*Continued*)

Height of the Ridiculous, The . . . . . . . . . 104
Old Friend, The . . . . . . . . . . . . . 147
Old Ironsides . . . . . . . . . . . . . . 197
Home . . . . . . . . . . . . . . . . . . 121
Home on the Range . . . . . . . . . . . . . 254
Home, Sweet Home . . . . . . . . . . . . . 111
HOPKINSON, JOSEPH (1770-1842)

Hail, Columbia . . . . . . . . . . . . . 194
House by the Side of the Road, The . . . . . . . 270
*How dear to this heart are the scenes* . . . . . . . 208
HOWE, JULIA WARD (1819-1910)

Battle-Hymn of the Republic . . . . . . . . 230
How to Tell Bad News . . . . . . . . . . . 102


*I ain't afeard uv snakes* . . . . . . . . . . . . 64
I Am an American . . . . . . . . . . . . . 248
*I am not bound to win* . . . . . . . . . . . . 224
*I am ready to say to every human being* . . . . . . 193
*I am tired and sick of war* . . . . . . . . . . 241
I Believe . . . . . . . . . . . . . . . . 284
*I believe in the United States of America* . . . . . . 282
*I can't get 'em up* . . . . . . . . . . . . . 280
*I come from the city of Boston* . . . . . . . . . 251
*I do the very best I know how* . . . . . . . . . 224
*I'd Rather have Fingers than Toes* . . . . . . . . 120
*If all the world were candy* . . . . . . . . . . 19
*If a man can write a better book* . . . . . . . . 216
*If I read a book* . . . . . . . . . . . . . . 259
*If Nancy Hanks came back as a ghost* . . . . . . . 226
*If we do not make common cause to save* . . . . . . 224
*If you call a tail a leg* . . . . . . . . . . . . 225
*If you have hard work to do* . . . . . . . . . 113
*If you your lips would keep from slips* . . . . . . . 128
*I have not allowed myself to suppose* . . . . . . . 225
I Hear America Singing . . . . . . . . . . . 252
*I heard the bells on Christmas Day* . . . . . . . 228
*I know a place where the sun is like gold* . . . . . . 35
*I leave this rule for others when I'm dead* . . . . . . 203
*I like to see it lap the miles* . . . . . . . . . . 73
*I met a little Elf-man, once* . . . . . . . . . . 24

*I'm going out to clean the pasture spring* . . . . . . . 123
*In an ocean, 'way out yonder* . . . . . . . . . . 30
*I never Saw a Purple Cow* . . . . . . . . . . . 61
INGALLS, JOHN JAMES (1833-1900)
        Opportunity . . . . . . . . . . . . . . 265
Injun Summer . . . . . . . . . . . . . . . . 36
*In men whom men condemn as ill* . . . . . . . . . 251
In Ourselves . . . . . . . . . . . . . . . . 260
In School-Days . . . . . . . . . . . . . . . . 114
Inscription at Mount Vernon, The . . . . . . . . . . 191
Inscription on Plymouth Rock Monument, The . . . . . 165
Inscription on the Tomb of the Unknown Soldier . . . . 283
*In the future days which we seek* . . . . . . . . . 285
*I only regret that I have but one life* . . . . . . . . 186
*I pledge allegiance to the flag* . . . . . . . . . . 148
*I profess, sir, in my career hitherto* . . . . . . . . 214
*I shot an arrow into the air* . . . . . . . . . . 108
Is There a Santa Claus? . . . . . . . . . . . . 42
*I studied my tables over and over* . . . . . . . . . 57
It Couldn't Be Done . . . . . . . . . . . . . 135
*It doesn't breathe* . . . . . . . . . . . . . . 23
*I think that I shall never see* . . . . . . . . . . . 137
*It is a fearful thing to lead* . . . . . . . . . . . 276
*It is difficult to make a man miserable* . . . . . . . . 224
*It is easy enough to be pleasant* . . . . . . . . . . 145
*It is easy to find fault* . . . . . . . . . . . . . 268
*It is not raining rain for me* . . . . . . . . . . . 86
*It is the eternal struggle* . . . . . . . . . . . . 223
*It takes a heap o' livin' in a house* . . . . . . . . . 121
It Was . . . . . . . . . . . . . . . . . . 20
I've Been Workin' on the Railroad . . . . . . . . . 253
I Went to the Woods . . . . . . . . . . . . . 212
*I wish I was in de land ob cotton* . . . . . . . . . 227
*I wish to preach, not the doctrine* . . . . . . . . 275
*I wrote some lines once on a time* . . . . . . . . . 104

JACKSON, HELEN HUNT (1831-1885)
        October's Bright Blue Weather . . . . . . . . 118
JANVIER, MARGARET THOMSON (Margaret Vandegrift) (1845-1913)
        Sandman, The . . . . . . . . . . . . . . 72

JEFFERSON, THOMAS (1743-1826)
    Thou Art My Brother . . . . . . . . . . . . 193
    When a Man Assumes a Public Trust . . . . . . 193
Jeffries Wyman (*selection from*) . . . . . . . . . 257
Jest 'fore Christmas . . . . . . . . . . . . . . . 44
Jingle Bells . . . . . . . . . . . . . . . . . . 109
Judge Not . . . . . . . . . . . . . . . . . . . 251
June . . . . . . . . . . . . . . . . . . . . . 106
Justin Morgan Had a Horse (*selection from*) . . . . . . 198

*Keep conscience clear* . . . . . . . . . . . . . 168
*Keep thy shop* . . . . . . . . . . . . . . . . . 168
KEY, FRANCIS SCOTT (1779-1843)
    Star-Spangled Banner, The . . . . . . . . . 199
Kicker, The (*selection from*) . . . . . . . . . . . 265
KILMER, JOYCE (1886-1918)
    Trees . . . . . . . . . . . . . . . . . . 137
KING, BEN (1857-1894)
    Pessimist, The . . . . . . . . . . . . . . 269

*Labor to keep alive* . . . . . . . . . . . . . . 165
Ladder, The . . . . . . . . . . . . . . . . . . 112
Ladder of Saint Augustine, The (*selection from*) . . . . . 142
Landing of the Pilgrim Fathers, The . . . . . . . . 163
LARCOM, LUCY (1824-1893)
    Brown Thrush, The . . . . . . . . . . . . 22
*Laugh, and the world laughs with you* . . . . . . . 129
LAZARUS, EMMA (1849-1887)
    New Colossus, The . . . . . . . . . . . . 264
LEE, HENRY (1756-1818)
    First in War, First in Peace . . . . . . . . . 191
LEE, ROBERT E. (1807-1870)
    Farewell to His Army . . . . . . . . . . . 240
Lend a Hand . . . . . . . . . . . . . . . . . 122
Letter from the Alamo, A . . . . . . . . . . . . 202
Letter to Mrs. Bixby . . . . . . . . . . . . . . 239
Let Us Be of Good Cheer . . . . . . . . . . . . 204
*Let us have faith that right makes might* . . . . . . . 224
Let Us Raise a Standard . . . . . . . . . . . . 186
Liberty and Union . . . . . . . . . . . . . . . 214

LIEBERMAN, ELIAS (1883-    )
    I Am an American . . . . . . . . . . . . . 248
*Life? and worth living* . . . . . . . . . . . 272
Life, a Question . . . . . . . . . . . . . 272
*Life has loveliness to sell* . . . . . . . . . . . . 91
Life on the Ocean Wave, A . . . . . . . . . . 204
Limericks . . . . . . . . . . . . . . . 110
LINCOLN, ABRAHAM (1809-1865)
    Eternal Struggle, The . . . . . . . . . . 223
    Gettysburg Address, The . . . . . . . . . 238
    Letter to Mrs. Bixby . . . . . . . . . . . 239
    Sayings . . . . . . . . . . . . . . . 224
    Second Inaugural Address (*selection from*) . . . . . 239
Lincoln-Douglas Debates (*selection from*) . . . . . . 223
*Listen, my children, and you shall hear* . . . . . . . 174
Little Boy Blue . . . . . . . . . . . . . 41
*Little drops of water* . . . . . . . . . . . . 32
Little Elf-Man, The . . . . . . . . . . . . 24
Little Gustava . . . . . . . . . . . . . . 39
Little Orphant Annie . . . . . . . . . . . . 46
Little People, The . . . . . . . . . . . . . 49
Little Things . . . . . . . . . . . . . . 32
Little Willie . . . . . . . . . . . . . . 73
Little Word, A . . . . . . . . . . . . . . 112
Living . . . . . . . . . . . . . . . . 267
LONGFELLOW, HENRY WADSWORTH (1807-1882)
    Arrow and the Song, The . . . . . . . . . . 108
    Arsenal at Springfield, The . . . . . . . . . 222
    Building of the Ship, The (*selection from*) . . . . 219
    Charles Sumner (*selection from*) . . . . . . . 253
    Children's Hour, The . . . . . . . . . . . 26
    Christmas Bells . . . . . . . . . . . . 228
    Day Is Done, The . . . . . . . . . . . . 96
    Elizabeth (*selection from*) . . . . . . . . . 136
    Evangeline (*selections from*) . . . . . . 123, 132
    Forest Primeval, The . . . . . . . . . . . 123
    Hiawatha's Childhood . . . . . . . . . . . 155
    Hiawatha's Sailing . . . . . . . . . . . . 158
    In Ourselves . . . . . . . . . . . . . 260
    Ladder of Saint Augustine, The (*selection from*) . . . 142
    Mills of God, The . . . . . . . . . . . . 144

LONGFELLOW, (*Continued*)

    Paul Revere's Ride . . . . . . . . . . . . 174
    Poetic Aphorisms (*selection from*) . . . . . . 144
    Poets, The (*selection from*) . . . . . . . . 260
    Psalm of Life, A . . . . . . . . . . . . . 131
    Rainy Day, The . . . . . . . . . . . . . 130
    Sail On, O Ship of State . . . . . . . . . . 219
    Santa Filomena (*selection from*) . . . . . . . 139
    Ships That Pass in the Night . . . . . . . . 136
    So When a Great Man Dies . . . . . . . . 253
    Stars, The . . . . . . . . . . . . . . . 132
    Success . . . . . . . . . . . . . . . . 142
    Village Blacksmith, The . . . . . . . . . . 262
    Whene'er a Noble Deed Is Wrought . . . . . 139
*Look at a branch, a bird, a child, a rose* . . . . . . . 95
*Look out how you use proud words* . . . . . . . . 122
Look Up . . . . . . . . . . . . . . . . . 115
Lost . . . Forever . . . . . . . . . . . . . 205
*Lost, yesterday, somewhere between* . . . . . . . . 205
LOVEMAN, ROBERT (1864-1923)
    April Rain . . . . . . . . . . . . . . . 86
LOWELL, JAMES RUSSELL (1819-1891)
    Aladdin . . . . . . . . . . . . . . . . 85
    Be Noble . . . . . . . . . . . . . . . 217
    First Snow-Fall, The . . . . . . . . . . . 98
    Fourth of July Ode . . . . . . . . . . . . 192
    Glance Behind the Curtain, A (*selection from*) . . . 260
    Hands of Toil, The . . . . . . . . . . . . 260
    Jeffries Wyman (*selection from*) . . . . . . . 257
    June . . . . . . . . . . . . . . . . . 106
    Let Us Be of Good Cheer . . . . . . . . . 204
    Once to Every Man and Nation . . . . . . . 221
    Present Crisis, The (*selection from*) . . . . . . 221
    Stanzas on Freedom (*selection from*) . . . . . 220
    They Are Slaves Who Fear . . . . . . . . 220
    To the Dandelion . . . . . . . . . . . . 37
    Vision of Sir Launfal (*selection from*) . . . . . 106
    Wisdom . . . . . . . . . . . . . . . . 257

MANN, HORACE (1796-1859)
    Lost . . . Forever . . . . . . . . . . . . 205

Man Without a Country, The (*selection from*) . . . . . . 196
Marines' Song, The . . . . . . . . . . . . . . . 277
*Mary had a little lamb* . . . . . . . . . . . . . . 59
Mary's Lamb . . . . . . . . . . . . . . . . . 59
MASON, CAROLINE ATWATER (1853-1939)
      En Voyage . . . . . . . . . . . . . . . . 94
*Master of human destinies am I* . . . . . . . . . . 265
Maud Muller (*selection from*) . . . . . . . . . . 93
McCUTCHEON, JOHN T. (1870-1949)
      Injun Summer . . . . . . . . . . . . . . . 36
McGUFFEY'S PRIMER
      Mary's Lamb . . . . . . . . . . . . . . . 59
      Work While You Work . . . . . . . . . . . 58
McGUFFEY'S SECOND READER
      Beautiful . . . . . . . . . . . . . . . . 38
McGUFFEY'S THIRD READER
      Little People, The . . . . . . . . . . . . . 49
      Persevere . . . . . . . . . . . . . . . . 38
      Pert Chicken, The . . . . . . . . . . . . . 119
      Sunset . . . . . . . . . . . . . . . . . 77
McGUFFEY'S FIFTH READER
      How to Tell Bad News . . . . . . . . . . . 102
Melancholy Days, The . . . . . . . . . . . . . . 105
Melting Pot, The (*selection from*) . . . . . . . . . 252
*Merrily swinging on brier and weed* . . . . . . . . . 70
Merry Sunshine . . . . . . . . . . . . . . . . 66
Mess Call . . . . . . . . . . . . . . . . . . 281
MILLER, JOAQUIN (1841-1913)
      Byron (*selection from*) . . . . . . . . . . . 251
      Columbus . . . . . . . . . . . . . . . . 153
      Judge Not . . . . . . . . . . . . . . . . 251
Mills of God, The . . . . . . . . . . . . . . . 144
*'Mid pleasures and palaces though we may roam* . . . . . 111
*Mine eyes have seen the glory* . . . . . . . . . . . 230
Miracles . . . . . . . . . . . . . . . . . . 258
Miriam (*selection from*). . . . . . . . . . . . . 216
Miss Mehitabel's Son (*selection from*) . . . . . . . 266
Modern Hiawatha, The . . . . . . . . . . . . . 91
Monroe Doctrine, The . . . . . . . . . . . . . 201
MONROE, JAMES (1758-1831)
      Monroe Doctrine, The . . . . . . . . . . . 201

MOORE, CLEMENT C. (1779-1863)
    Visit from St. Nicholas, A . . . . . . . . . . . 78
MORLEY, CHRISTOPHER (1890-    )
    Animal Crackers . . . . . . . . . . . . . . . 23
MORRIS, GEORGE POPE (1802-1864)
    Woodman, Spare That Tree . . . . . . . . . 146
Mortifying Mistake, A . . . . . . . . . . . . . . 57
Motto . . . . . . . . . . . . . . . . . . . . . 203
Mountain and the Squirrel, The . . . . . . . . . . 56
*My country, 'tis of thee* . . . . . . . . . . . 190
My Face (limerick) . . . . . . . . . . . . . . . 110
My Nose . . . . . . . . . . . . . . . . . . . 23
My Old Kentucky Home . . . . . . . . . . . . . 211
My Symphony . . . . . . . . . . . . . . . . . 266

Nancy Hanks . . . . . . . . . . . . . . . . . 226
Nathan Hale . . . . . . . . . . . . . . . . . 183
Nathan Hale Said . . . . . . . . . . . . . . . 186
NATHAN, ROBERT (1894-    )
    Daughter at Evening, The . . . . . . . . . . 21
National Flag, The . . . . . . . . . . . . . . . 247
Nation's Strength, A . . . . . . . . . . . . . . 218
New Colossus, The . . . . . . . . . . . . . . 264
New Moon, The . . . . . . . . . . . . . . . 60
*No man is born into the world whose work* . . . . . . 260
Nonsense Jingles . . . . . . . . . . . . . . . 92
*Not gold, but only man can make* . . . . . . . . 218
*Nothing great was ever achieved* . . . . . . . . 213
*Nothing to do but work* . . . . . . . . . . . 269
No Time Like the Old Time (*selection from*) . . . . . 147
*Not in the clamor of the crowded street* . . . . . . 260
*Not like the brazen giant of Greek fame* . . . . . . 264
Now . . . . . . . . . . . . . . . . . . . . 113
*Now not a window small or big* . . . . . . . . . 95
*Now, that is the wisdom of a man* . . . . . . . . 213
*Now the sun is sinking* . . . . . . . . . . . . 77

*O beautiful for spacious skies* . . . . . . . . . 286
"*O bury me not on the lone prairie!*" . . . . . . . 256
O Captain! My Captain! . . . . . . . . . . . . 242
October's Bright Blue Weather . . . . . . . . . . 118
*Of course what we have a right to expect* . . . . . . 273

[ 307 ]

*O give me a home, where the buffalo roam* . . . . . . . 254
*Oh! the old swimmin'-hole!* . . . . . . . . 116
Old Folks at Home . . . . . . . . . . . 210
Old Friend, The . . . . . . . . . . . 147
Old Ironsides . . . . . . . . . . . . 197
Old Oaken Bucket, The . . . . . . . . . . 208
Old Swimmin'-Hole, The . . . . . . . . . 116
O Mother of a Mighty Race . . . . . . . . . 206
Once to Every Man and Nation . . . . . . . . 221
*Once when the snow of the year* . . . . . . . . 76
On Digital Extremities . . . . . . . . . . 120
*One of the most striking differences* . . . . . . . 268
*One on God's side* . . . . . . . . . . . 218
On Freedom of Thought . . . . . . . . . . 182
*On my honor I will do my best* . . . . . . . . 149
*On my honor, I will try* . . . . . . . . . 149
Open Wood-Fire, An . . . . . . . . . . . 266
Opportunity (Braley) . . . . . . . . . . 130
Opportunity (Ingalls) . . . . . . . . . . 265
O'REILLY, JOHN BOYLE (1844-1890)
       What Is Good? . . . . . . . . . . 141
Origin of the Forget-Me-Not, The . . . . . . . . 32
Or Make a Better Mousetrap . . . . . . . . . 216
*O say, can you see, by the dawn's early light* . . . . 199
*O sun and skies and clouds of June* . . . . . . . 118
*O The Raggedy Man! He works fer Pa* . . . . . . 54
*Our band is few, but true and tried* . . . . . . . 185
Our Country . . . . . . . . . . . . 279
*Our Country is a tapestry* . . . . . . . . . 279
Our Country, Right or Wrong . . . . . . . . 223
*Our fathers fought for Liberty* . . . . . . . . 192
Our Hired Girl . . . . . . . . . . . . 52
Our Lips and Ears . . . . . . . . . . . 128
*Our reliance is in the love of liberty* . . . . . . . 225
Out to Old Aunt Mary's . . . . . . . . . 124
*Out where the handclasp's a little stronger* . . . . . 255
Out Where the West Begins . . . . . . . . 255
*Over hill, over dale* . . . . . . . . . . 278
*Over the river and through the wood* . . . . . . . 62

PAGE, WILLIAM TYLER (1868-    )
    American Creed, The . . . . . . . . . . . 282
PAINE, THOMAS (1737-1809)
    These Are the Times that Try Men's Souls . . . . 173
PALMER, T. H.
    Try, Try Again . . . . . . . . . . . . . 77
PARLEY, PETER (see Samuel Griswold Goodrich)
Pasture, The . . . . . . . . . . . . . . . 123
Paul Revere's Ride . . . . . . . . . . . . . 174
PAYNE, JOHN HOWARD (1791-1852)
    Home, Sweet Home . . . . . . . . . . . 111
PEATTIE, DONALD CULROSS (1898-    )
    Bird Music (from An Almanac for Moderns) . . . 85
Pedigree . . . . . . . . . . . . . . . . . 137
Persevere . . . . . . . . . . . . . . . . . 38
Pert Chicken, The . . . . . . . . . . . . . 119
Pessimist, The . . . . . . . . . . . . . . . 269
PHILLIPS, WENDELL (1811-1884)
    Eternal Vigilance . . . . . . . . . . . . 218
    One on God's Side . . . . . . . . . . . . 218
PIERPONT, JOHN (1785-1866)
    Jingle Bells . . . . . . . . . . . . . . 109
    Warren's Address . . . . . . . . . . . . 180
    Whittling . . . . . . . . . . . . . . . 148
POE, EDGAR ALLAN (1809-1849)
    Bells, The . . . . . . . . . . . . . . . 99
Poetic Aphorisms (selection from) . . . . . . . . 144
Poetry . . . . . . . . . . . . . . . . . . 259
Poets, The (selection from) . . . . . . . . . . 260
Poor Richard's Almanack (selections from) . . . . . . 168
PRATT, ANNA MARIA
    Mortifying Mistake, A . . . . . . . . . . 57
Preamble to the Constitution . . . . . . . . . . 187
Prelude to Evangeline, The . . . . . . . . . . 123
Present Crisis, The (selection from) . . . . . . . . 221
Primer Lesson . . . . . . . . . . . . . . . 122
Psalm of Life, A . . . . . . . . . . . . . . 131
Pudd'nhead Wilson's Calendar . . . . . . . . . 268
Purple Cow, The . . . . . . . . . . . . . . 61

Rabbit, The . . . . . . . . . . . . . . . . 58

Raggedy Man, The . . . . . . . . . . . . . . . . 54
Railway Train, The . . . . . . . . . . . . . . . . 73
Rainy Day, The . . . . . . . . . . . . . . . 130
Rapid Progress of True Science, The . . . . . . . . 186
READ, THOMAS BUCHANAN (1822-1872)
      Sheridan's Ride . . . . . . . . . . . . . 235
Reading makes a full man . . . . . . . . . . . . . 169
Reveille . . . . . . . . . . . . . . . . . 280
RICHARDS, EDWARD HERSEY (1874-    )
      Wise Old Owl, A . . . . . . . . . . . . 61
RICHARDS, LAURA ELIZABETH (1850-1943)
      Difference, The . . . . . . . . . . . . 24
Riches . . . . . . . . . . . . . . . . . 209
RILEY, JAMES WHITCOMB (1849-1916)
      Little Orphant Annie . . . . . . . . . . 46
      Old Swimmin'-Hole, The . . . . . . . . 116
      Our Hired Girl . . . . . . . . . . . . 52
      Out to Old Aunt Mary's . . . . . . . . 124
      Raggedy Man, The . . . . . . . . . . . 54
      When the Frost Is on the Punkin . . . . . 138
Roads . . . . . . . . . . . . . . . . . . 144
Robert E. Lee's Farewell to His Army . . . . . . . 240
Robert of Lincoln . . . . . . . . . . . . . . 70
ROBERTS, ELIZABETH MADOX (1886-1941)
      Hens, The . . . . . . . . . . . . . . 33
      Rabbit, The . . . . . . . . . . . . . . 58
ROBINSON, CORINNE ROOSEVELT (1861-1933)
      Life, a Question . . . . . . . . . . . . 272
ROBINSON, EDWIN ARLINGTON (1869-1935)
      Eternal Partnership . . . . . . . . . . . 95
Rock-A-By Lady, The . . . . . . . . . . . . . 48
ROCKEFELLER, JR., JOHN D. (1874-    )
      I Believe . . . . . . . . . . . . . . . 284
Rock Me to Sleep . . . . . . . . . . . . . . 125
ROELOFSON, EMILY BRUCE (1841-1921)
      Origin of the Forget-Me-Not, The . . . . . . 32
ROOSEVELT, FRANKLIN DELANO (1882-1945)
      Four Freedoms, The . . . . . . . . . . 285
ROOSEVELT, THEODORE (1858-1919)
      Speak Softly and Carry a Big Stick . . . . . . 275
      Strenuous Life, The . . . . . . . . . . 275

Roosevelt, (*Continued*)
    To the Boys of America . . . . . . . . . . . 273
    We Stand at Armageddon . . . . . . . . . . 275
    When You Play, Play Hard . . . . . . . . 275
Rule, A . . . . . . . . . . . . . . . . . 165
Runaway, The . . . . . . . . . . . . . . . 76

Sail On, O Ship of State . . . . . . . . . . 219
Salute to Our Flag . . . . . . . . . . . . 148
Sandburg, Carl (1878-    )
    Fog . . . . . . . . . . . . . . . . 98
    Primer Lesson . . . . . . . . . . . . . 122
Sandman, The . . . . . . . . . . . . . . 72
Santa Filomena (*selection from*) . . . . . . . 139
Sargent, Epes (1813-1880)
    Life on the Ocean Wave, A . . . . . . . . 204
Sayings of Abraham Lincoln . . . . . . . . 224
Sayings of "Poor Richard" . . . . . . . . . 168
Schurz, Carl (1829-1906)
    Our Country, Right or Wrong . . . . . . . 223
Second Inaugural Address, The (*selection from*) . . . . . 239
Seein' Things . . . . . . . . . . . . . 64
Shaw, Henry Wheeler ("Josh Billings") (1818-1885)
    Kicker, The (*selection from*) . . . . . . . 265
    Wheel That Squeaks, The . . . . . . . . 265
*She frowned and called him Mr.* . . . . . . . 110
Sheridan's Ride . . . . . . . . . . . . . 235
Sherman, William Tecumseh (1820-1891)
    War . . . . . . . . . . . . . . . 241
Ships That Pass in the Night . . . . . . . . 136
Sick Call . . . . . . . . . . . . . . . 280
*Silently, one by one, in the infinite meadows* . . . . . 132
Sill, Edward Rowland (1841-1887)
    Baker's Duzzen uv Wize Sawz, A . . . . . . 90
*Sir, I would rather be right* . . . . . . . . 200
Skinner, Charles R. (1844-1928)
    Now . . . . . . . . . . . . . . . 113
Smith, Samuel Francis (1808-1849)
    America . . . . . . . . . . . . . . 190
Snow-Bound . . . . . . . . . . . . . . 126
Snow-Storm, The . . . . . . . . . . . . 140

Solitude . . . . . . . . . . . . . . . . . . 129
*Somebody said that it couldn't be done* . . . . . . . . 135
Song of Hiawatha (*selections from*) . . . ·. . . . 155, 158
Song of Marion's Men . . . . . . . . . . . 185
Song of Milkanwatha, The (*selection from*) . . . . . 91
*So nigh is grandeur to our dust* . . . . . . . . . . 86
"Sonnets" IV . . . . . . . . . . . . . . . 217
*Soupy, soupy, soupy* . . . . . . . . . . . . 281
So When a Great Man Dies . . . . . . . . . . 253
Speak Gently . . . . . . . . . . . . . . 129
Speak Softly and Carry a Big Stick . . . . . . . 275
Stable Call . . . . . . . . . . . . . . . 281
*Stand! the ground's your own* . . . . . . . . . 180
Stanzas on Freedom (*selection from*) . . . . . . . 220
Stars, The . . . . . . . . . . . . . . . 132
Star-Spangled Banner, The . . . . . . . . . 199
Steady Gain of Man, The . . . . . . . . . . 250
*Still sits the schoolhouse by the road* . . . . . . . 114
Strenuous Life, The . . . . . . . . . . . . 275
STRONG, GEORGE A. (1832-1912)
      Modern Hiawatha, The . . . . . . . . . . 91
Success . . . . . . . . . . . . . . . . . 142
Sugar-Plum Tree, The . . . . . . . . . . . 67
SUMNER, CHARLES (1811-1874)
      National Flag, The . . . . . . . . . . . 247
Sunset . . . . . . . . . . . . . . . . . 77
Sunset on the Bearcamp (*selection from*) . . . . . . 134

Tall Oaks from Little Acorns . . . . . . . . . 55
Taps . . . . . . . . . . . . . . . . . 281
TEASDALE, SARAH (1884-1933)
      Barter . . . . . . . . . . . . . . . 91
*Tell me not, in mournful numbers* . . . . . . . . 131
Ten Little Injuns . . . . . . . . . . . . . 80
Ten Times One Is Ten (*selection from*) . . . . . . 115
Thanatopsis (*selection from*) . . . . . . . . . 136
Thanksgiving Day . . . . . . . . . . . . 62
THAXTER, CELIA (1835-1894)
      Little Gustava . . . . . . . . . . . . . 39
THAYER, ERNEST LAWRENCE (1863-1940)
      Casey at the Bat . . . . . . . . . . . . 88

*The American continents . . . are henceforth* . . . . . . 201
*The axe has cut the forest down* . . . . . . . . . 205
*The axis of the earth sticks out visibly* . . . . . . 217
*The best business you can go into* . . . . . . . . 254
*The breaking waves dashed high* . . . . . . . . 163
*The Constitution, in all its provisions* . . . . . . . 215
*The day is cold, and dark, and dreary* . . . . . . . 130
*The day is done, and the darkness* . . . . . . . . 96
*The fisher who draws in his net too soon* . . . . . . 38
*The fog comes on little cat feet* . . . . . . . . . 98
*The following anecdote is a case in point* . . . . . 166
*The gingham dog and the calico cat* . . . . . . . 34
*The little toy dog is covered with dust* . . . . . . . 41
*The melancholy days are come* . . . . . . . . . 105
*Them ez wants, must choose* . . . . . . . . . . 90
*The morns are meeker than they were* . . . . . . . 87
*The mountain and the squirrel had a quarrel* . . . . . 56
*The night was coming very fast* . . . . . . . . 33
*The outlook wasn't brilliant for the Mudville nine* . . . . 88
*The pedigree of honey* . . . . . . . . . . . 137
*There are hermit souls that live withdrawn* . . . . . . 270
*There is a homely old adage which runs* . . . . . . 275
*There is a just God who presides* . . . . . . . . 172
There Is Always a Best Way . . . . . . . . . 141
*There is no friend like the old friend* . . . . . . . 147
There Is No Frigate Like a Book . . . . . . . . 145
*There is the National flag* . . . . . . . . . . 247
*There's a merry brown thrush sitting* . . . . . . . 22
There Was a Little Girl . . . . . . . . . . 31
*There was an old man of Nantucket* . . . . . . . 110
*There was a tree stood in the ground* . . . . . . . 81
*There was once a pretty chicken* . . . . . . . . 119
*The rosy clouds float overhead* . . . . . . . . 72
These Are the Times That Try Men's Souls . . . . . 173
*The snow had begun in the gloaming* . . . . . . . 98
*The sun has sunk behind the hills* . . . . . . . . 27
*The sun shines bright in the old Kentucky home* . . . . . 211
*The sun that brief December day* . . . . . . . . 126
*The time is now near at hand* . . . . . . . . . 182
*The time to hear bird music* . . . . . . . . . 85
*The use of money* . . . . . . . . . . . . 168

*The wheel that squeaks* . . . . . . . . . . . . . 265
*The wisest man could ask no more* . . . . . . . . 257
*The world must be made safe* . . . . . . . . . . 276
*The Yankee boy, before he's sent to school* . . . . . 148
They Are Slaves Who Fear . . . . . . . . . . . 220
*They say a reasonable amount o' fleas* . . . . . . . 101
*This is the forest primeval* . . . . . . . . . . 123
*This is the story of a common ordinary* . . . . . . . 198
*This monument marks the first burying ground* . . . . 165
Thomas Jefferson Said . . . . . . . . . . . . 193
THOREAU, HENRY DAVID (1817-1862)
    Go Confidently . . . . . . . . . . . . . 209
    I Went to the Woods . . . . . . . . . . 212
    Riches . . . . . . . . . . . . . . . . 209
    Walden (*selections from*) . . . . . . . . 209, 212
Thou Art My Brother . . . . . . . . . . . . 193
*Though the mills of God grind slowly* . . . . . . . 144
*Though we travel the world over* . . . . . . . . . 213
*Thou, too, sail on, O Ship of State* . . . . . . . . 219
Three Hundred Thousand More . . . . . . . . . 231
Three Little Kittens, The . . . . . . . . . . . . 68
*'Tis a lesson you should heed* . . . . . . . . . . 77
*'Tis fine to see the Old World* . . . . . . . . . . 261
To Achieve Greatness . . . . . . . . . . . . 251
*To drum-beat and heart-beat* . . . . . . . . . . 183
To Find the Beautiful . . . . . . . . . . . . 213
*To him who in the love of Nature holds* . . . . . . 136
*To live content with small means* . . . . . . . . . 266
*To Look up and not down* . . . . . . . . . . 115
To the American Troops before the Battle of Long Island . 182
To the Boys of America . . . . . . . . . . . . 273
To the Dandelion . . . . . . . . . . . . . . 37
*To the People of Texas and All Americans* . . . . . . 202
*To think I once saw grocery shops* . . . . . . . . 133
*To touch the cup with eager lips* . . . . . . . . 267
*Touched by a light that hath no name* . . . . . . . 134
*Training is everything* . . . . . . . . . . . . 268
TRAVIS, WILLIAM BARRET (1809-1836)
    Letter from the Alamo, A . . . . . . . . . 202
Trees . . . . . . . . . . . . . . . . . . 137
Try, Try Again . . . . . . . . . . . . . . 77

*Truth, crushed to earth, shall rise again* . . . . . . . . . . 241
Truth, the Invincible . . . . . . . . . . . . . . . 241
TWAIN, MARK (Samuel L. Clemens) (1835-1910)
    Father's Education . . . . . . . . . . . . . . 101
    Pudd'nhead Wilson's Calendar . . . . . . . . . 268
*'Twas the night before Christmas* . . . . . . . . . . 78

*Under a spreading chestnut-tree* . . . . . . . . . . 262
*Under a toadstool crept a wee Elf* . . . . . . . . . . 50
UNTERMEYER, LOUIS (1885-    )
    Young Mystic, The . . . . . . . . . . . . . 63
*Up from the meadows rich with corn* . . . . . . . . 232
*Up from the South, at break of day* . . . . . . . . 235

VANDEGRIFT, MARGARET (see Margaret Thomson Janvier)
VAN DYKE, HENRY (1852-1933)
    America for Me . . . . . . . . . . . . . 261
    Four Things . . . . . . . . . . . . . . 271
VEST, GEORGE G. (1830-1904)
    Eulogy of the Dog . . . . . . . . . . . . 100
Village Blacksmith, The . . . . . . . . . . . . 262
Vision of Sir Launfal, The (*selection from*) . . . . . . 106
Visit from St. Nicholas, A . . . . . . . . . . . 78
Voluntaries (*selection from*) . . . . . . . . . . . 86

Walden (*selections from*) . . . . . . . . . . 209, 212
Wanted (*selection from*) . . . . . . . . . . . 220
War . . . . . . . . . . . . . . . . . . . 241
Warren's Address . . . . . . . . . . . . . . 180
WASHINGTON, GEORGE (1732-1799)
    Be Courteous to All . . . . . . . . . . . . 171
    Let Us Raise a Standard . . . . . . . . . . 186
    Rule, A . . . . . . . . . . . . . . . . 165
    To the American Troops before the Battle of Long
      Island . . . . . . . . . . . . . . . 182
*Washington, the brave, the wise, the good* . . . . . . 191
*Wasn't it pleasant, O brother mine* . . . . . . . . . 124
*Way down upon de Swanee Ribber* . . . . . . . . 210
*We are coming, Father Abraham* . . . . . . . . . 231
Wendell Phillips Said . . . . . . . . . . . . 218
*We are not so sensible of the greatest health* . . . . . . 168

WEBSTER, DANIEL (1782-1852)
  God Grants Liberty . . . . . . . . . . . . . . 203
  Liberty and Union . . . . . . . . . . . . . . 214
WEEMS, MASON LOCKE (Parson) (1759-1825)
  George Washington and the Cherry Tree . . . . . 166
*We fight in honorable fashion for the good* . . . . . . 275
*We have not wings, we cannot soar* . . . . . . . . 142
Well, Did You Hear? . . . . . . . . . . . . . . 196
*Were a star quenched on high* . . . . . . . . . 253
*Were half the power that fills the world* . . . . . 222
*We sat together close and warm* . . . . . . . . . 63
WESCOTT, EDWARD NOYES (1847-1898)
  Fer a Dog . . . . . . . . . . . . . . . . . 101
*We search the world for truth* . . . . . . . . . . 216
We Stand at Armageddon . . . . . . . . . . . . 275
*We take pleasure in answering at once* . . . . . . . 42
We Thank Thee . . . . . . . . . . . . . . . 28
*We, the People of the United States* . . . . . . . . 187
What Do We Plant? . . . . . . . . . . . . . 143
What Is Good? . . . . . . . . . . . . . . . 141
*What is more cheerful, now* . . . . . . . . . . . 266
"*What is the real good?*" . . . . . . . . . . . 141
Wheel That Squeaks, The . . . . . . . . . . . 265
*When a man assumes a public trust* . . . . . . . . 193
Whene'er a Noble Deed Is Wrought . . . . . . . . 139
*When Freedom from her mountain height* . . . . . 187
*When he came to tuck me in* . . . . . . . . . . 20
*When, in the course of human events* . . . . . . . 181
*When I was a beggarly boy* . . . . . . . . . . 85
*When I was a boy of fourteen* . . . . . . . . . 101
When Johnny Comes Marching Home . . . . . . . 243
When the Frost Is on the Punkin . . . . . . . . 138
*When they said the time to hide was mine* . . . . . 58
*When to the flowers so beautiful* . . . . . . . . . 32
*When you play, play hard* . . . . . . . . . . . 275
*When you've got a thing to say* . . . . . . . . . 267
*Whichever way the wind doth blow* . . . . . . . . 94
"*Which is the way to Baby-land?*" . . . . . . . . 51
WHITTIER, JOHN GREENLEAF (1807-1892)
  Barbara Frietchie . . . . . . . . . . . . 232
  Barefoot Boy, The . . . . . . . . . . . . . 29

WHITTIER, (*Continued*)

    Bible, The . . . . . . . . . . . . . . . . 216

    Chapel of the Hermits, The (*selection from*) . . . 250

    For of All Sad Words . . . . . . . . . . . 93

    In School-Days . . . . . . . . . . . . . 114

    Little People, The . . . . . . . . . . . . 49

    Maud Muller (*selection from*) . . . . . . . . 93

    Snow-Bound . . . . . . . . . . . . . . 126

    Steady Gain of Man, The . . . . . . . . . . 250

    Sunset on the Bearcamp (*selection from*) . . . . . 134

WHITMAN, WALT (1819-1892)

    By Blue Ontario's Shore (*selection from*) . . . . . 251

    I Hear America Singing . . . . . . . . . . 252

    Miracles . . . . . . . . . . . . . . . 258

    O Captain! My Captain! . . . . . . . . . . 242

    To Achieve Greatness . . . . . . . . . . . 251

Whittling . . . . . . . . . . . . . . . . . 148

*Why, who makes much of a miracle?* . . . . . . . 258

WILCOX, ELLA WHEELER (1850-1919)

    Solitude . . . . . . . . . . . . . . . . 129

    Worth While . . . . . . . . . . . . . . 145

Wilderness Is Tamed, The . . . . . . . . . . . 205

*Willie saw some dynamite* . . . . . . . . . . . 73

WILSON, WOODROW (1856-1924)

    Congress Is Asked to Declare War . . . . . . . 276

    World Must Be Made Safe, The . . . . . . . 276

Wind and the Leaves, The . . . . . . . . . . . 65

Wisdom . . . . . . . . . . . . . . . . . . 257

Wisdom of a Man, The . . . . . . . . . . . . 213

Wise Old Owl, A . . . . . . . . . . . . . . 61

*With a pick and with a shovel* . . . . . . . . . 281

*With doubt and dismay you are smitten* . . . . . . 130

*With malice toward none* . . . . . . . . . . . 239

Woodman, Spare That Tree . . . . . . . . . . 146

Woodrow Wilson Said . . . . . . . . . . . . 276

WOODWORTH, SAMUEL (1785-1842)

    Old Oaken Bucket, The . . . . . . . . . . 208

Words for Army Bugle Calls . . . . . . . . . . 280

Work While You Work . . . . . . . . . . . . 58

Worth While . . . . . . . . . . . . . . . . 145

Wynken, Blynken, and Nod . . . . . . . . . . 74

Yankee Doodle . . . . . . . . . . . . . . . 170
*Yep, sonny, this is sure enough Injun summer* . . . . . 36
*Yet, sometimes glimpses on my sight* . . . . . . . . 250
*You can fool some of the people* . . . . . . . . . 225
*You'd scarce expect one of my age* . . . . . . . . 55
Young Mystic, The . . . . . . . . . . . . . 63
*"Youngster, let that show you* . . . . . . . . . . 196
Your Country . . . . . . . . . . . . . . . 196

ZANGWILL, ISRAEL (1864-1926)
    Great Melting Pot, The . . . . . . . . . . . 252

PRINTED IN U.S.A.